THE MIRACLE CHILD

Out of darkness into His light
Broken Wings To Flight

RICHARD B. SIMMONS

Published by LBFWorld Publishing
Houston, Tx

THE MIRACLE CHILD
ISBN 978-1-946430-00-7

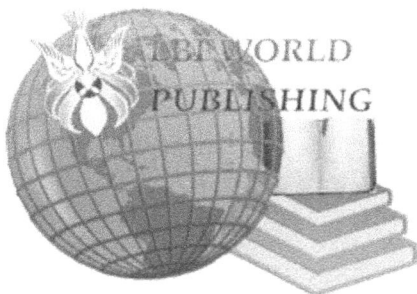

Printed in USA by LBFWorld Publishing
PO Box 1198
Porter, Tx 77365
lbfpublishing.com

Dedication

I dedicate *The Miracle Child* To My deceased father Edward Neal Cox. Thank you for the dance of a lifetime! We went through valleys and mountains, but came out in victory. Thank you for being my father, even though, you had no commitment to do so! I love you dad and can't wait to see you in Heaven on my appointed day by the Lord.

My amazing mother Cynthia Cox, we to have had our challenges, but the Lord has always been right there with us. Thank you for your continued love and support through my most challenging times in life. My love for you mom is immeasurable.

Thank you to the mighty servants of God who responded to the call to intercede tirelessly: my sister Mellisa Cox Holt and my Aunt Tina Stitt! Thank you to all those who intervened in my path to help me walk out of darkness into His glorious light! Janice Costa, if you would not have entered into my life, I can say I would not be here today! Thank you so much!

Last but never least, the way you would want it, to my dear deceased spiritual mother "Mama Mig" Marjorie Bodine. Thank you for pouring so much into me of the prophetic and the Holy Spirit. I dearly miss our daily prayers and conversations. You lit a fire in me that I will take forth for God's Glory. Love you Mama Mig!

Thank you sincerely, from the depth of my heart, to everyone else that is not named. God used a lot of you to help me get here. I love you all and am grateful! I am blessed to have so many people to respond to God's call and pour into my life. The Lord richly bless each of you in overflow in Jesus Mighty Name.

Table of Contents

Foreword

Many people write books out of revelation or by what they feel, but here is somebody who came through the storms of life. What I call a "Severe Hurricane Survivor" and his name is Richard Simmons, and he put's a Powerful Tool in the World's hands to show what a Yes I can person can do even when all the odds are against him. How to turn the lemons of life into lemon aid and realize without Gods Power and salvation humanity has no hope.

Out of this life changing, mind restoring tool, The Miracle Child there comes hope in a person's life to know if God can do it for Richard He can do it for anybody else. If I can bring Biblical reference to it, it would be this is for somebody out there trying to come out of a Storm in life. The Miracle Child is a roadmap a Chart on life's Journey to show us; nothing is impossible with God when we allow God to get involved.

We can make it as Champion Overcomers and World Changers on this journey called life. This tool will activate Hope and Hope brings Expectations and High Expectations makes us tap into Heavens resources and no longer live a life of only existing but a Life of Significance. As you read, you will see and understand more of God's love, and God's transforming power and that you can do exceedingly and abundantly above what we can ever ask or pray for as all things are possible for those who believe.

Dr. Gustav Du Toit
Apostle Lofdal International, Cape Town, South Africa
DrGustavDuTuit.Com

It is a great pleasure to write this forward for Apostle Richard's first book. I knew the book would be a great blessing, but at the time I could not see the full magnitude of this book. If I had to summarize this book in one sentence, I would say: this is a book about radical faith in both life and his Apostolic Mandate.

This is not a preachy or holier than thou book but a soul-bearing story of a man God set aside from the moment he was in his mother's womb.

The Story chronicles Apostle Richard's troubled and often misunderstood childhood, the ups and downs of a life outside of the full knowledge of the grace of God. Thank God the story does not end there. The author cleverly took us through his troubled life first to then leave us on a faith high by sharing with us how God saved him by recounting the many of the miraculous instances where God showed up and showed off in his life and in the ministry mandate that he has been called to; Lead by Faith Ministries.

The entire book really highlights the 1 Corinthians 1:27-29 verses:

27 But God has selected [for His purpose] the foolish things of the world to shame the wise [revealing their ignorance], and God has selected [for His purpose] the weak things of the world to shame the things which are strong [revealing their frailty]. 28 God has selected [for His purpose] the insignificant (base) things of the world, and the things that are despised and treated with contempt, [even] the things that are nothing, so that He might reduce to nothing the things that are, 29 so that no one may [be able to] boast in the presence of God.

So if you have a past, have fallen short once, twice or three hundred thousand times (let's be honest, who has not?) then, by all means, pick up this book and read how the transformative grace and power of the Holy Spirit can transform your past and mold it into an amazing asset for the kingdom of God.

Catherine Storing

confidenceunchained.org

Acknowledgements

Mom – Thank you for your never ending love and for believing in me when I could not believe in my self. You have always and will always be my hero .

Edward N. Cox (Dad) – Though our lives traveled through many dark and very demonic places the Lord sent His angel for both of us. You were my father by choice and I will forever be grateful. I love you dad and cannot wait to be reunited again in Heaven.

"Mama Mig" Marjorie Bodine – To have had a spiritual mother like you was Gods divine plan. You helped shape my spiritual life tremendously. You finally got it through to me "Let go and Let God". I am looking forward to seeing you again in Heaven. You gave God 92 years of selfless obedient service.

Aunt Tina Stitt and sister Mellisa Cox Holt – Thank you for years of intercessory prayer, patience and unconditional love.

Brian Shepherd – Thank you for your dedication to the Lords work, and everything you do for me and the ministry. You are a blessing from the Lord a great teacher, man of God, and servant. I am thankful you are on our team and as spiritual family!

Janice Kelly Costa – How many times I have questioned if you were an angel from the Lord. The 29 years you have been in my life with wisdom, love and direction. Honestly you are a second mother to me. Thank you for your patience and understanding. The days and nights of listening. God used you mightily and I can say had He not put you in my life I would not be here on this earth today. I love you and thank you!

Joshua, Mario, Marco and Jonathan – I have been blessed for the many years of fathering each of you in this world. My heart and love is never ending for each of you. I have experienced the hurt, rejection and pain like each of you. As a father I understand the outburst, anger, walls, and tears. My prayer is that you fully receive God's unconditional love and surrender to His perfect plan in you lives. Thank you for allowing me to be a father figure in your life. It has been one of the greatest parts of my life!

Dr. Gustav Du Toit – Thank you for taking me under your wing. I am honored and continue to learn so many things every time we have traveling across america and in team ministry together. You inspire me, and I am truly thankful for your heart and passion for the Lords work. You are one a in a million in the body of Christ, but also in the ministry, and this is evident with the hundreds of weeks of true authentic real revival at Lofdal in South Africa. To sum it up you are "The authentic real man of God". You will never understand the depth of my gratitude to you. Thank You!

Jon Simmons – We to have had our up's and downs dealt to us in this life, and had our own differences and challenges, but you are my brother and I will always love you. Thank you for everything you have done for me and the ministry. One day you will preach the gospel for Jesus Christ! Love you brother!

Ron Simmons – The road point forward toward the Lord. I am thankful God has brought restoration to our relationship. You are my biological father, and I do love you very much. I am thankful for the past chapters in our life being closed and reconciled and for the great plans God has for our future. God bless you!

Lenin, Amarilis, and Hernandez family – I thank God for my Honduran family in the Lord. Serving God with you all has been a real experience. I love you all and look forward to the many years ahead.

Catherine Storing – Wow our divine meeting took me from prophetic words over my life to actually writing this book. I am thankful to the Lord God for bringing us together, and your amazing coaching, and support in writing. You truly brought forth a greater confidence. Thank you for you awesome "confidence unchained ministry"!

To everyone in the path of my destructive years – I look now and see the blessing. Thank you. Many of you caught a side of me that was wounded, confused, broken, hurt and scared. If I have not personally apologized please accept this apology for any hurt and pain I caused you. I ask you to please forgive me and know God has created a new man for His Glory!

To all who have abused, and hurt me over the many years – Please know I hold nothing against each of you. I choose to forgive each of you and part ways in love. Please find deliverance, peace and love in Jesus Christ. He delivers, saves and heals. I bless each of you and pray you fill the perfect plan God has for your life in Jesus.

To all of the other amazing and dear people in my life – you have nor been forgotten or less important. I thank God for your life, and the times we have had in the Lord. Bless you all!

Introduction

Light and dark are a clear divide as are the ways of Heaven and earth. The Miracle Child is the story of my life from brokenness, rejection, abuse, and hopelessness before Christ to a transformation that continues to go forth until Glory. Learning to love and trust again, over come and surrender to the Lord's glorious plan are the fruits of this book. I pray this book will help you to "Let go and Let God". You may be trying to understand someone in your life or you may be going through this storm. Either way I know you divinely are reading this book and I declare breakthrough in your life in Jesus name! Many professionals, and people have communicated to me that my life is a miracle and by the normal I would not be where I am today. I will tell you it is by the hand of God almighty through the blood of Jesus Christ, and the power of the Holy Spirit that I survived, and overcame.

Revelation 12:11 says it best "And they overcame him by the blood of the Lamb and by the word of their testimony, and they did not love their lives to the death."

PART 1
A Childhood to remember

CHAPTER 01

THE ✘ MIRACLE CHILD

A Rough Beginning

FROM A ROUGH START

It was an expected day to come—it was a date set for my birth; a day to I would be birthed and enter this world. That date, – June 28, 1973—it had was prearranged that at 10 o'clock a.m, It would be early by C-section at the hospital in Amarillo, Texas. Everybody was excited! My mother was ready, and all systems were go. She was taken into the delivery room and prepared for a c-section delivery. My mom describes lying on the table, and she felt like an elephant had stepped on her chest. As a result, she was in tremendous pain. From the very onset, the enemy was out to cancel my life, even if that meant taking my mother out in the process. The story goes on, in this rough beginning, as I was born and coming into this earth, many challenges, trials, and tribulations would unfold. It was all for God's glory. My mother describes going through days, trying to recover from the birth. She felt as if her life had been drained out of her.

On the second day, they brought me in to be fed by her. She recalls that I was kicking her in the stomach as hard as I could. Anger arose in her, and we were off to a rough start. Of course, my mother loved me tremendously and still does to this day. As the days went forth, she held me tight and close. She took good care of me. We had a very close bond. The violence occurring in my new world would be a thing that brought on a level of fear in my life. It was ultimately the plan of the enemy to stop me from fulfilling God's plan, but God had plans of his own.

As I was growing up, there was much violence inflicted by my biological father Ron on my mother. It ultimately had a negative effect on her, my brother, and me. One day, Ron slapped my mother on her ear, causing a period of hearing loss. In a rebellious rage, he jerked me out of her hands and departed the house with me to go hang out with his friends. My mother, in utter desperation, made many phone calls enquiring about our whereabouts. She finally tracked him down and begged him to return me home so that I could be fed and nurtured. Eventually, he returned me to my mother.

The same anger, rage, and abuse continued to unfold through my infancy years into my childhood. My father left my mother, brother, and me. After he had left us, we weren't in the best position financially or emotionally. We were left with the old run down Volkswagen bug. It constantly leaked water and always seemed to be on the edge of falling apart and breaking down.

A NEW BEGINNING

One day, as a very young boy, I remember a new man appearing on the scene. I called him Ed. That was his name. I didn't know what to think about him, and honestly, I didn't know what he thought about me. It was confusing and in fact, it was all pretty new, but he was there, and I made the best of it. I do recall, as he moved in with us at our house at Estacado subdivision in Amarillo, Texas, he brought some sweet dishes along with him.

As a young man, I was in an unusual situation. I was coping with a lot of confusion and rejection with my father gone. With a new man in our home, I probably wasn't the friendliest person in accepting him into our home in the beginning. In fact, one day I recall telling him, in a small disagreement, "You can take your dishes and leave if you don't like it around here." But honestly, he seemed like a pretty okay guy, and we began to tolerate each other pretty well. In fact, you could probably say; we started to bond a little.

He worked in the insulation industry dealing with refineries mostly. He was in the sales department of the business. One morning, as our little family was forming, I recall Ed coming in and playing on my little record player, "You are my sunshine, my only sunshine. You make me happy when skies are gray. You'll never know dear how much I love you. Please don't take my sunshine away." It seemed like things were heading off into a fresh breath and a new start and that something might be stable in my life.

I CAN TRUST YOU. RIGHT?

In our new beginning as a family, in our house at Estacado, I had a babysitter who took care of me. I was a trusting young boy at this point in life. She brought me to my room and told me that we were going to play a game called 'Doctor.' As she moved my bed down to cover the door in my bedroom, she then undressed me and began to do very unhealthy things with me. I remember, as a young child, reflecting upon this, and thinking, 'I trust her, this seems a little strange, but she won't do me any harm.'

As we were in the midst of playing Doctor's Office, there was banging on the door. I hear a frantic voice – that of my mother—on the other side of the door, demanding the door be opened immediately. I remember the shock flowing through my body and mind thinking "What is happening here? Why is my mother so upset?" Until this point, it all seemed innocent to me. I was doing as I was told. The look on the babysitter's face was one I will never forget. In haste, the nanny made rapid movements to move the bed out of the way and get my clothes back on my body. The babysitter opened the door. There, with a very frantic angry look on her face, my mother stood on the left side of the door, and she began to unleash a verbal wrath of fury on the babysitter. The hand of the devil was working, trying to bring destruction at such a young age. My mother escorted the babysitter up the hallway towards the front door. I remember looking into my brother's room, which was one room past mine and hearing him laugh with a look on his face. It was a dark look —almost a "welcome to the club" look. My brother hadn't had the easiest life growing up either, due to his biological father.

Time seemed to pass by, and thoughts of the event appeared to go away. One afternoon, I was out playing, and I saw the babysitter coming down the sidewalk. I rejoiced and ran towards her as I was so glad to see her. She turned away from me and did not want to be seen with me. I'll never forget the feeling of being rejected as she did not want to speak with me, and wondering, "Why are you doing this? What did I do to cause this?" I don't remember seeing her after that, but I do remember placing a letter I wrote her with crayons in the envelope. I wrote her name on it and put it in the post office box, thinking it would reach her. A day later, the postman returned it to our home. I was sad and very disappointed.

I was a timid young fellow, trying to figure life out at this early age of five. I remember the day we had that family meeting. We were called together in the living room and informed we were making a move to Houston, Texas.

CHAPTER 02

THE **MIRACLE CHILD**

Dark Doors Opening

OFF TO THE SPACE CITY

As we relocated to Houston, Texas, we found our new home at the Memorial Orleans apartments in the beautiful area of the town. I just knew in my heart that this move would be a new beginning. It was going to bring new hope and hopefully some peace. As we moved into our apartment, I rejoiced looking at the room and thinking about how our family was going to come together and grow in peace. The room was empty and ready to build a new life.

My stepfather Ed had received a raise and was now the vice-president of sales at the insulation company. Though everybody was jubilant about it, that increase brought an increase in pressure for him. He began drinking. As the drinking increased, the anger and frustration in the house increased and hopes of peace and unity began to break apart and fall away. Once again, violence was erupting in our home. My stepfather took me and threw me through the air across the room. I tried to make an escape up the stairs, but I was caught and put in more physical and verbal abuse. My brother arose and came to my rescue by confronting my stepfather. My brother gave me an exit to flee temporarily to the safety of my room.

The abuse continued. The drinking continued. Happiness

was no place inside. In fact, this was becoming the norm. I recall frequently going on bike rides at the park, connected to our apartment, to find such a place of safety and silence.   I was incredibly lonely, as friends in my life were far and few between.

DARK DOORS WERE OPENING

One evening, as my parents were out of the apartment, I was being watched by my brother in our apartment on the second floor. He had some friends over. We were all hanging out in the living room as they broke out an ouija board and began to summon spirits of darkness. I didn't think too much of it until demonic things started to take place on the ouija board— movement, etcetera— and then a demon manifested in the hallway, walking toward us. The fear that was already alive in my life went to a whole different level.

Days passed, and not much was said about that dark experience, but I knew deep inside of me, something had shifted, and it wasn't a good thing. Feelings of anger, rage, wanting to hurt people began to fill me at that young age of 7 years old. In fact, I even had thoughts of going and hurting an infant child at one of my brother's friends' apartment there in our complex. Thank God that never happened, but the thought plagued me.

As the days, weeks and months progressed, I began looking up to my brother. I started to see even deeper things going on with my brother in his life— drugs and sexual promiscuity involving other girls— Seeds were being planted in my life that was bringing a very wrong view and wrong understanding of what love and friendship are. The reality is that no one in our family knew what love was. It was all about survival. With my innocence being ripped away from me at such a young age, there was no love or innocence that I had ever known. It left a tremendous void in my heart.

THE LIVABLE FOREST

We once again arrived at a new season in life as we moved to a new place again. It seemed like we were always moving. This time, we made a move to The Woodlands, Texas. Again, there was a glimmer of hope that things would change for the better as we are moving to a new place. We moved into a house on the golf course, living next to a prominent football player. I knew that new things were in store. It was a great house with many windows, a fantastic kitchen, even a garden terrain in the middle of the house. We had to be set this time for success! We had a great home in a great neighborhood... Right?

We all felt so perfect at the time, but would it last? One afternoon, my mother and I were out on a wooden deck on the back portion of the house where she was doing some planting and gardening. She enjoys plants and does quite well with them. She was wearing a Levi's that have been cut off into shorts. It had strings that were hanging off of them. Growing up in a poverty spirit as a child, amongst many other things, I honestly didn't know any different or any better clothing standards. My stepfather Ed came out in a fit of rage, screaming and cussing at my mother. A great afternoon in the outdoor sun turned immediately into a war. I felt helpless. I wanted to defend her but didn't know how.

As Ed made her remove those cutoff Levi's there in the living room; mom looked defeated and broken. He took the cut off Levis while screaming, flung the garage door open and threw them into the garage. Hope began to diminish once again. I always blanked these things out as a child and just focus on the good times and not the bad.

LET'S PLAY BALL

On another note, things appeared to be improving as I was gaining a few friends. One of my new friends, Ryan, played soccer and his father was the coach of the soccer team. He invited me to join them on the team. There was a nervous excitement in me, but I made the choice that I would join the team. I wasn't the all-star soccer player but I was a part of the team, and for that, I was thankful and happy. It felt different to be accepted, to be wanted in the context of the team. You see, I'd come from a place of not being accepted or wanted in anything. In fact, I was defeated!

One afternoon, we went to our soccer practice as we routinely did. Evidently, Ryan's father had said something about my stepfather's drinking to my stepfather and the topic of discussion had arisen in our living room. I was the guilty one that day. I remember having such a fear I was paralyzed. The screaming and cussing between my mother and stepfather were just that, and I was in the middle. A short time later, Ryan's father showed up at our home to pick me up for soccer practice and authoritatively told my stepfather that he was taking me to soccer. The side door of the house was opened, and I took a cautious exit and went directly to their van. I sat in the back of the van looking out the rear window. I was pondering the whole way thinking if I was responsible and should have kept my mouth shut. It was a good feeling to have somebody to stand up for me. I went on through the day as if nothing had happened, and hoping it would just go away.

As the days passed by, the soccer season finished. I didn't see much of my stepfather at the house anymore. His working hours were increasing which led to increasing in his drinking.

The violence at our home was increasing as well. I spent as much time away from home as possible.

ARE YOU OUT TO HURT ME?

One day I visited the neighbor's house. Nobody was home. Their family cat sat on a chair on their back porch. I approached the cat cautiously and sat there for a few moments wanting to pet it. As I began to caress the cat's head and ears, the cat started to purr, and fear got the better of me. I backed away with a racing heart and ran to my mother expressing that the cat was going to attack me. When she asked what had happened exactly, I told her. She explained to me that the cat wasn't trying to hurt me, but it was rather expressing a sense of love and satisfaction. However, what was love? It was very hard for me to understand or comprehend.

HEY LOOK AT ME!

As the time moved along, I began to take notice of my brother receiving far more attention. My parents gave my brother much more gifts. Even though it hurt my heart, I didn't hold it against him and my parents. I just chose to let it be.

A new level of unhealthy thinking had surfaced as I watched my brother. I continued to observe and overhear my brother talking about what he would do with them and to them. It was a little strange to me, and there was a lot of confusion going on in my head. My family members had opened doors of sexual abuse to me at the age of seven. At this point, this continued path of my life of darkness and destruction was just starting to open up to a new place.

One afternoon, my friends Bryan, Ryan, and me, were planning an adventurous trip to the woods with a young lady from our neighborhood, a couple of days later. We had all agreed that we would have sexual relations with her and she agreed to it. We were way too young to be involved in this stuff, but we were like- monkey see monkey do. In preparation for this trip, we took a pillow cover to the local drug store in The Woodlands Wharf. It is a local mall. As Ryan talked to the clerk, Bryan and I proceeded to take cigarettes and other items that we would need for the journey into the woods. Our intentions were of a sexual nature of course. You could see the seeds of wickedness continuing to grow due to observing the different seeds planted in our young life. We had been taken advantage of at some point in life.

As that day arrived, we all went to the woods with the pillow and the sleeping bag. That was more of an actual performance than action. We were trying to act like adults and do the things that we had seen. We were not even at the age to physically execute our plan. In this time, I began to notice a lot of confusion about who I was and what God had planned for me to be?

GO WITH HIM

One afternoon, while playing in my room, my brother had a friend over. My brother put forward the idea that I should spend some time with his friend. He was being nice to me and giving me attention which I was not used to having. His friend took me to my mother and my father's restroom and sexually molested me. He was very smooth in his talk and offered to bring me little gifts to open a door for another experience. His offers reoccurred several times until one day I finally stopped. I knew deep within me that this was not right, and began to avoid him. However, I could not find the power in me to say no. He eventually stopped coming around.

Till this point of my life, I think that I was used to focusing on the good things and bearing the wrong, not realizing that one day in the future, they would have to be reconciled or dealt with mentally. The confusion was coming to a whole new level in my life, and my identity as a person was very unclear. I remember the day I felt in the depth of me the sense of right and wrong as I was there at Bryan's home. His mother was in the room sitting on the chair as we were on the floor watching TV. Bryan and I began to enter a new level of unhealthiness with thoughts about sexuality. You could say a lot of role play started to stir. Nothing came out of it, outside of some touching and talking; but nonetheless, the enemy's plan was in action to advance and continue to bring destruction, ultimately, to kill me.

DEMONIC ENCOUNTER BEHIND THE SCHOOL

I recall one afternoon at my elementary school in The Woodlands going out to a wooded area. It turned to a strange small opening which led to an open circular area where the trees had been cleared. I felt spiritually led out there, but not in a right way. Something present there was trying to pull me to a place of darkness in the spiritual realm. I departed that area of the woods, knowing that I had just encountered the devil's kingdom. I knew something was very in-depth and dark there.

LET'S MOVE TO THE LAKE

Soon after, by the grace of God, we moved yet once again. Life took us to Atascocita, Texas where we lived in The Pine Shores Subdivision. Having a fraction of hope, I was somewhat excited. We moved to a lovely home just down the street from Lake Houston. At this point, my stepfather Ed was the executive vice-president of the insulation company. We were living a pretty decent life at this stage regarding money, and what it could provide. We would eat out every night at restaurants, and we lived in an amazing home spread over two stories, comprising of four bedrooms, a large living room, and a beautiful backyard.

I'm about ten years old at this point. I am in the fifth grade attending the Timber's Elementary School. I made several good friends there. I was coming to a new place in life while the old thoughts had become a thing of the past, at least at the current state of mind.

I entered a new rebellious stage toward adults while still fostering a profound aspect of wanting to please everyone and always have the answers. I yearned to be accepted, always to try to have the answer, the solution. I was at the age where I wanted a special girl for me; yes, a girlfriend. There were several girls in the neighborhood I had approached, and we had come close too. I found myself sabotaging the relationships every time. It wasn't due to their looks, likes or anything else; the problem was within me. They were too intimate with me, and I couldn't have that, even though a big part of me wanted to have someone special. I noticed that I did not like being touched by them.

DARK EERIE NIGHT

I recall the times getting darker and deeper. Some nights, my stepfather would be in complete darkness in the living room sitting on his chair, as if not knowing where to go or what to do? It seemed that he was at a hopeless point in his life. I would always have the eeriest feeling being in the living room with him in the dark. There was this sense of something present in the room that I could not see. Looking back, it was the spirits of oppression, depression, and suicide. These were driving Ed deeper into an ocean of darkness and alcohol was the island that he thought would save him.

Little did I know that the devil was trying to take him to a deeper, darker place as well. The family as a whole was heading into a deeper spiral.

AFTER SCHOOL EVICTION

One day I arrived home from school, and there was an 18-wheeler from my stepfather's work sitting in front of our house. I was met by a man with a badge and a gun in the front yard. They walked me to my room and told me to pack my room. We were moving once again. What differed this time, we had no place to go and no place to call home. Our friends across the street, David and Karen, and their son Jimmy gave us a refuge and a temporary place to stay with while all of our belongings were taken to my stepfather's work and put into the warehouse until we could find a new house.

As we stayed with our friends, we realized that David was an alcoholic and smoked like a chimney. One night I had gone to bed on the couch to get some sleep for another day at school. I was awoken by the fire department personnel coming through the living room carrying David's mattress. It had caught fire as he had fallen asleep with the cigarette in his hand. I wondered, "Is this how everyone lives?"

Jimmy and I were caught in beginning days of MTV Airing on cable TV. These were the days of back to back music videos no other real programming. Jimmy took me to his room and began to show me some Hip Hop records and began to explain how it was about rhymes and proceeded to share a rap record. While having a slight interest, it didn't take a deep pull at me at this point in life, but the seed was planted.

NO LONGER REFUGEES

One day after school a family news flash occurred. We were going to be moving down the road to a new two-story house—a house just across from the neighborhood pool near the park. This time, my step-sister Melissa and step brother Barrett were going be moving in with us. It was bringing an exciting twist and hopefully a new beginning. As we lived there, it seemed to be a good start. Family life was going on, and everyone had their fortress. Everybody was doing what they were doing, and things seemed all well. It was nice to see differing themes in everyone's rooms. My Melissa's room was always in great shape, with Rick Springfield playing on the radio.

As time progressed, we're the happy go lucky family with my brother and sister living the great American dream. One day they had to leave. It was an unexpected departure as their mother had gone to court and brought them back to live in Odessa, TX. Things digressed rapidly after their departure. To compound the issue, my brother and I hooked up illegal cable TV to our home. Our actions caught up with my stepfather Ed at 3 o'clock one day. A massive beating on the door commenced with the words, "Police! Police!". The door was opened and my stepfather Ed was taken into custody. Obviously, he had much anger and rage and many words protruding out his mouth at the top of his lungs as they took him away. Part of me honestly was euphoric that he was gone, but another part of me knew that there was going to be a price to pay.

When he returned home, it was far from cute or silent. The violence went to a new level, and there was a darkness that was unfolding with his increased drinking.

DEMONIZED TO DELIVERED

My stepfather Ed would laugh at times, and when he would

laugh, the deepest fear filled the atmosphere. I would become paralyzed, and the hair on my arms would stand up from the feeling of this demonic laugh. This laugh was from the demons possessing him. I tried my best to stay away from the house as much as possible to avoid him and the demons.

Not knowing much about God being present or not, I could tell you this for sure that the devil was present in that house. A little time later, my friend Christopher's mother, who was a Christian, came to our home. I recall my stepfather screaming to my mother, "Get those *#^$#& Christians off my property now!" This scream was not a typical scream. This was the devil talking through my stepfather. "Get those *#^$#& Christians out of here!" There were some creative words that he said that we couldn't publish in this book.

Not long after that, I convinced my mother to let me leave the craziness of that home and go on to stay with my friend Christopher and his family. I feared for my mom but could not live in that crazy situation anymore. It was strange to find such peace to be sleeping on his floor and not listening to constant screaming or being concerned about what would happen next. It seemed astonishing that life was so uneventful at Christopher's home. Dinner was served at the same time every day, people would sit around the table, there was prayer at the table, and no one screamed or argued. I wondered if this was what life is supposed to be?

At some point, my stepfather made a choice to stay with his mother and father in Midland, TX. They were Pentecostals, filled with the Holy Spirit. As he left, my mom had no choice but to get a job. She went to become a cashier at the local Wal-Mart superstore, and I returned to live at home with her.

The house went from having several people living there to just me and my mother. Many times, I would stay there alone at night as my mom had no choice but to work. I recall a field next to us. In the house, I had an awareness of the demons. They would torment and plague me. I would call my mother at Wal-Mart and beg her to come home. The season of stability had ended: the nice cars, eating out every night, and even hope had fully diminished. In fact, even having food at home was far and few between in these days. One day my mother left Wal-Mart after the break to bring me a chicken sandwich from Burger King and had to return to work immediately. As soon as she departed, one of my brother's friends who was there took my lunch from me to eat it.

HOME ALONE

It was interesting to see the transition of friends as life was changing from having family around to just feeling completely alone. When my brother would show up, he would typically be involved with drugs, females, and chaos. I found myself wanting to be alone away from people. I guess because people usually brought hurt, disappointment, and pain. Realizing everyone was not the same would become be something I would realize very late.

PART II

A New Dimension

CHAPTER 03

There Is a God

PRAYER OF A RIGHTEOUS MAN

I remember my stepfather Ed, became gravely ill when we lived on the Dunlevy Street here in Houston. I was in my room working on a computer that we found in the trash on the curbside in the neighborhood. We did not have the money to buy the things I had an interest in, such as computers and electronics. I desired to learn more and grow through a hands-on approach, because learning through traditional means was always tough for me as I had ADHD. I was in my room looking at the wires and thinking about the flow, structure and function of this old broken down computer system when my mother came into my room and said that my stepfather Ed was in bad shape. As I walked into the other room where my stepfather and mother were resting on their bed, you could see death dawning upon him. There was blood coming from his nose and mouth, and his skin was wet and ashy pale.

We weren't close to the Lord at that time in life, but we knew he was very real due to various incidents. At that point, my mother said that I should go and call Larry Gatlin, who was a friend of my stepfather Ed from earlier years. He was in the Gatlin Brothers Band—a country music band and is a Christian man of faith. I picked up a faith-based book on which Larry Gatlin, at some point, had written his phone number so my stepfather could contact him. I called the number written in the book and reached Larry Gatlin. I began to speak to this man wondering if he might just hang up on me or be unavailable. I began to explain to him that I was Ed Cox's son and that we were waiting for an ambulance to arrive. My dad was dying. He began to speak with such love and peacefulness; I could tell he cared about what was happening. This call impacted me profoundly and planted seeds that would grow and flourish through the years ahead. Larry spoke to me about Jesus Christ and that Jesus was the only intervention and answer to this problem. We needed a miracle, and it was in the Lord Jesus Christ. Larry offered to pray with me about my father's declining health situation. I agreed, and as he prayed, I felt something change! I felt deep down that something had changed and I knew God was there. We hung up, but his words about Jesus Christ and his love never left. That night Larry was a light in a very dark place. I now had a hope that I had not felt in a long time. After hanging up the phone, my mother came into the kitchen when I had just got off the phone with Larry, and she told me that it was time—it was time to call the ambulance because my dad was dying. She looked very shocked and scared. I believe we were facing a hopeless situation, but I was holding on to the recent meeting with Jesus I had just gained from Larry's prayer. As I picked up the phone again, I remembered the conversation I just had with Larry Gatlin and the prayer that he had prayed about my stepfather. I had a mustard seed of faith and did not know how it was going to happen, but there was a profound hope that my dad would be okay. I picked up the phone and called the 911 emergency center for an ambulance to rush to our home. I remember the various questions that never seemed to end. I was feeling every second tick by knowing they counted and were important because my stepfather was lying lifeless in the other room dying. Blood was coming out of his body and he had internal bleeding. I will never forget the yellow eyes and a pale gray complexion all over his body.

The 911 operator finally informed me that an ambulance was en route. Every minute for which I just waited there for the ambulance felt like an eternity. I felt helpless again. I was trying to find mercy for my stepfather who had always been so hateful and filled with rage. I went to the front of the house on the street, awaiting the arrival of the ambulance. It seemed like hours were passing quickly. I pondered if they got lost, or maybe they did not get the message to come, perhaps... As I was waiting, in desperation I began to call out to God and asked him for help. I remembered bargaining with God that night, not knowing him, and saying, "God, we've been so bad. We've been full of anger. I hope you will please help us; we need your help!" Imagine these words coming out of the mouth of a twelve-year-old. I was bargaining with God, hoping and believing, for a little chance, that it would move the ear and the hand of God to send down his angels to help us in our situation and our time of need.

As I sat there and cried out and bargained with God, I heard a thought in my head, "Why are you doing this? This person is the man who has beaten you, beaten your mother!" Something in me still pulled, still desired to help him. It was a feeling of not wanting anyone to go through this.

From a distance, I could hear the siren approaching and shortly around the corner, came the red flashing emergency lights. As the head lights were flashing and coming closer to me, I was blinded when the ambulance pulled up. I just stood there in a state of shock. The gravity of the situation was becoming more real every moment. The ambulance's paramedic approached me and asked, "Do you need the ambulance?" and I said "Yes! My father is dying. He's bleeding."

I guided the paramedics into our yard, and we rushed to the house. I stood at a distance in the living room observing the medics starting to take rapid evasive action. They started IV's in his arms, put an oxygen mask over his mouth and nose, and attached the heart monitors. There was such quickness in their movements. It was evident there was a serious problem with my dad. They were tossing furniture and other things in the room out of the way. My stepfather was fading away even more by each passing minute and could not answer their questions. They placed him rapidly on the gurney and wheeled him right out. My mother was trying to help but looked so scared and frantic. As they loaded him into the ambulance, my mom got in the back of the ambulance with him. The paramedic who was driving asked me if I'd like to ride in the front and I did. I was scared and numb. As I sat there in a rigid state, knowing the situation was outside of any control I could even try to have, I heard the paramedic's voice call out to me. I came out of a state of looking out at nothing. Some call it the 50-yard line stare. I answered him "Yes." The paramedic asked, "Can you help me?", And I agreed. He showed me the siren switch and had me operate the siren on the way to the hospital. In a strange way, it took my mind off the situation a little bit and brought some peace in the process. As we arrived at the Hermann Hospital Emergency Department, they rushed to take my stepfather into the shock trauma area. This room is where the urgent cases are taken, and many times people leave this earth. I sat in the emergency department waiting area in a comatose state, thinking "Here comes another failure, another loss. What will we do next?" There was little to no stability in our life as I was growing up. It seemed like a continuous struggle to survive.

That night, my dad was admitted to the intensive care unit at Hermann Hospital. Hours later, we were permitted to go in and see him. He laid there in a gown with tubes to his mouth and nose. There were multiple poles with many differing medication drips and pumps. The sound of the medical helicopter landing next to the ICU was frequent. The coming days and weeks turned into many hours in the waiting rooms, pondering many thoughts back and forth, and total uncertainty. One late night, we received a call to come into the hospital. We could not afford to park in the parking lot, so we parked around by the Houston Zoo. We walked along the dark street. Many homeless people and beggars lived there. I felt too eerie. We made it by the grace of God and went up to the intensive care unit. They placed a football helmet on him. Tubes were coming to his nose, down his throat, and to each arm, and poles and poles of IV machines, breathing machines and heart monitors.

The nurse informed my mother and me that night that when they put the football helmet on people in the intensive care unit, they typically don't make it out alive. For weeks, he sat in there. For weeks, he laid in that bed with the football helmet on. Many machines were assisting him, but my mom and I refused to give up hope. Then he was moved to a different part of the intensive care unit.

I learned the rights and wrongs, the do's and don'ts of biohazards, putting on gowns, gloves, and masks. The doctors were informing us often that there was only a little chance that he would make it. I sat in a room with multiple doctors saying the same things so many times, but strangely my dad kept pulling through by a thread. I would see them call out code blue in the ICU many times, and a lot of people were not making it. I knew God had His hand on my dad. One night, mother and I were in the ICU, and the doctors informed us that my dad was

37

going to die in the next 24 hours, and we needed to call in the family. As we went home in a defeated state, my mother sat down at the kitchen table and started making phone calls to my dad's mother, sister and previous wife. I went to my room and just pondered on the situation and again asked God to help. The next day the family arrived and gathered in the waiting room downstairs. I had been up stairs at my dad's bedside. He was unconscious, had dry and chapped lips and mouth with the breathing tube. I refused to accept what the doctors were saying! I went back down the elevator to arrive at the lobby and made my way to the waiting area where I overheard my family discussing burial plans. I screamed out loud at them in anger "My dad is not dead, so we are not burying him right now!" I went back upstairs and soon, my aunt Bonnie arrived with a lady she had met downstairs in the waiting room. Bonnie and the woman walked into the isolation room to pray for my dad. There were only two people allowed at a time, but the nurses had formed a special bond with me and were giving me a special favor by letting me stay most of the time. As I stood outside the room; a multidimensional blue light came out of the top windows of the isolation room, and was a blue light I had never seen before and have never seen since. Shortly afterward, Bonnie and the lady walked out of the isolation suite. The woman came up to me and looked at me. As she looked into my eyes, I could feel something go into me. She said to me "son your father is going to be just fine. He is surrounded by the angels of the Lord. When she said this, there was such a feeling that came to me. That was God Almighty.

WINDOW OF OPPORTUNITY

The next afternoon, they said they had a small window of opportunity to take him to surgery, but he most likely would not make it through the surgery. I had made up my mind that I would not miss my dad's surgery. I was upset with my mother for going to work, and not being there, but honestly, she did the right thing. The next day, I arrived at the hospital hoping nothing had changed overnight, and he would still be going for his surgery. As I sat in his room, at 10 A.M, the surgical team came in to prepare my father and take him in for the surgery. As they wheeled him off on the gurney, I approached the point where I could no longer go with him. At a small distance, I saw them take my dad through a set of double doors. Immediately after the doors were shut, I was drawn to a clock on the wall and remember hearing this voice in my head "this is the time." I didn't have a relationship with the Lord at that point, but I was seeing His miracles happening around me right and left—His miracles to prevail. And I said, "God, take care of my dad. You can heal him. Hours later, the surgery was complete. The surgeons said that he wouldn't make it off the table, but he came out of the operating room alive. As they returned him to a new specialized intensive care unit, a whole new journey began- a trip of healing and restoration.

WE NEED A HOME, A MIRACLE

My mother and I, during this time, were facing challenges of the bills stacking up. The house rent became overdue, and we were facing homelessness once again. Knowing our eviction was on the way at any day, my mother began looking for another home for us. Many houses in the Westheimer area of Houston, Texas, have a lot of medical students, college students, and other renters. The price of many small apartments and houses is quite high. My mother looked and looked, and I could see one disappointment after another.

One night, I went with her to look at an apartment. It was tiny, but it had been fixed up to be an excellent unit, with beautiful wooden floors, nice crisp white paint, and decorative lighting. I sat there with my mom and thought, "Oh, what a beautiful place this is, quite small but what a wonderful home it would be," I felt safe there and could tell my mother liked it too. My mom asked for the price. And again, the price she gave was way out of our price range.

As the balloon once again began to deflate the strangest thing happened. The lady renting the small apartment could see the let-down on our face and the desperation quite honestly. She was hesitant but said "there may be another option. The neighbor next door has a duplex apartment. It's not quite as nice as this, but it's a safe, comfortable place." She walked us next door and introduced us to the man, his wife, and their baby. We thanked her, and she left. We found ourselves in a favorable position with this man and his wife, and they offered to show us the upstairs unit. I remember the lights working through an extension cord connected from the downstairs power outlet. Honestly, at this point, I didn't care if we had power or not. The extension cord didn't matter. We needed a roof over our head, a home. As we went up the dark stairs into this duplex and began to walk around, we realized that it was a nice size unit. The duplex had two bedrooms, a small dining room with a living room, a small office, a cozy kitchen with a shared shower and bathroom. It seemed too good to be true. I was expecting another disappointment at any moment. He asked for a deposit that we didn't have. He told us not to worry about it and that we could work it out. As my mother talked with the man about the monthly rent of the unit, he adjusted it. The rent fit right into our price range. Thank you, Jesus! We often talk about the many miracles of God that he has shown to us in our times of desertion and despair. Thank God for the new apartment. We were a day away from homelessness. So as we moved once again, this place wasn't the nicest by visual appearance, but it was safe, clean, comfortable, and was our new home.

We soon moved in, but I didn't see my mother much. She had been working many hours at her new job as a secretary at the Houston VA Medical Center. It was another miracle of God that they promoted her from a temporary contractor to a full-time employee. She was working in the chief of staff's office, and God had given her favor with Leonard Marcella who was her boss. Usually, they don't hire temporary employees; they have the practice to hire from within the VA Hospital. It was a far shot, but before they made the recommendation, we believed God and then God showed up. That job that the Lord gave my mother brought some stability, insurance, paid for our rent, and put food on our table. Oh, what a blessing God provided! He is never late, but we must trust and call out to Him.

DAY BY DAY

I was becoming quite a temporary resident of the Texas Medical Center here in Houston, Texas. I had a great understanding of the ins and outs of the medical center. The hours of the intensive care units gave me the opportunity to establish relationships with many of the employees from the cafeteria, ICU's, Doctors, nurses, and on throughout the hospital.

Little did I know that God had a bigger plan and he'd put the people unseen at the hospital that had the belief and the authority to speak life and break the chains over the situation in Jesus

Name.

LET'S TRY THIS AGAIN

My dad recovered, and the doctors had come to the point in his treatment where he could return home. It was a beautiful day when we were going to pick him up and bring him back. I remember us making our way to the exit, and I wished to stop by the front desk and introduce my father to the lady I had become friends with. I was so happy because the doctors had repeatedly said that he would die, but God had other plans!

We arrived at our home, and I felt that something was different about my father, Ed. I could not understand what it was, but something was different. I had forgiven him for everything in the hospital, and honestly, had nothing against him. We apparently were working on some broken pieces of the past. Little did I know that God had his hand in it.

He had gone through a procedure called a portacaval shunt which connected his portal vein and the inferior vena cava to give better blood flow to the lower parts of the body. This surgery was a result of his liver disease and cirrhosis caused by his alcohol abuse for many years. My father would drink a fifth of vodka daily. That's 1/5 of a US liquid gallon of vodka daily but never failed to take his vitamins. This was the main reason they had to operate on him, and it was no small operation.

My father had an incision all the way across his belly and the opening that was about 2.5" wide. These needed to be cleaned and re-bandaged daily. Typically, a home nurse would come and take care of this procedure, but we did not have one. I stepped up to the plate as I knew we needed to handle this. He told me not to worry about it, but there was no way he could do this, and I knew it. I was nervous because I always felt that everything I touched in life failed, and I was the reason. Something was different, and I decided to give it a go. This dressing changing and cleansing began to help us re-bond, and I liked it a lot!

BACK TO WORK

As the days progressed, my father was up and around. He wanted to get back to work, but his previous company had moved on during his years of sickness, and no longer had a place for him. In the past, he had sold insurance. So he made a choice to return to the insurance sales. It was not easy, but he accepted the challenge and re-entered the workforce.

CHAPTER 03: THERE IS A GOD

CHAPTER 04

THE MIRACLE CHILD

Off To The Mansion

About the age of 12, things were in a bad state financially. My stepfather was gone on a spiritual restoration journey and mother, and I moved in with my brother into the mansion. mansionIt had previously been occupied by a drug lord named "Big John."

The house had a huge meeting area that was a bar and a huge kitchen. There were a lot of secret areas in the house and secret escapes that were quite an impressive setup, to say the least. A common area was the huge living room with a big rock waterfall, a fish pond, and a massive fireplace. The rock walls formed around to the side with double doors that led to an enormous covered patio having a spa that could hold 24 people. There was a commercial barbecue pit that required a weight system to lift the solid steel lid. Situated across the street were a boat dock and its own private park.

An interesting story about this house—my brother came to occupy the house after the drug lord "Big John" who lived in it had committed suicide in the bar. Some of the blood splatters still existed on the wall.

THIS SPIRITUAL STUFF

I was at an exciting stage in life, having a great sensitivity to the spiritual things which I've had most of my life, but not understanding the difference between good and evil. At night, I would lay there and hear the footsteps coming down the hallway. When they arrived at my door, I would hear the wooden slats on the doors being touched one by one. I would hear the fingers run down the slats on the doors, but it did not bother me. There were times that I would sit in the spa and would hear the walking step by step up the wooden deck walkway toward the spa. Many nights, I would see translucent figures also.

To say the least, it became a routine part of my life. As for many years, I had the spiritual eyes to see these things, but I did not have the understanding that they were demonic and of the devil.

It was the night of 4th of July. My brother had organized a gathering of people for a special barbecue at the front area of the house. It had a massive wooden deck and many large trees. The trees had big lights that lit them up as well as the entire area. It was beautiful. As my brother was in the business of selling drugs through a pharmacy, he would insist on keeping the house locked up. The large lights in the trees unexpectedly went out. I, always looking for attention, would often do the things that irritated my brother, and usually got me in trouble. My brother instantly yelled out my name and was very upset with me, thinking that I had turned the light switch off from inside the house. The only problem with this scenario was that I didn't have the key. I assured him that I hadn't touched the light switch, so he gave me the key and sent me in to check the light switch and sure enough, it had been turned off. I turned it back on and went back out into the front deck area, locking the door behind. I returned the key to my brother and went on to the party. Not long afterward it happened again; yes the light went off again. This time he went in to discover the light switch was off and no one was inside.

I understood the existence of a spirit realm that was very real when I was very young. The understanding of the fullness of good and evil was yet to come.

Similar instances took place where we would be sitting around the bar area, talking, eating food and doing other activities. The ceiling fan above would stop rotating and would come to a slow stop. Then it would immediately begin rotating in the other direction. If you're familiar with ceiling fans, there's a small switch mounted there that has to be turned one way or another to control the direction of the fan. We would turn that switch back, and sure enough, the ceiling fan would go the other direction. It's kind of interesting, to say the least. It required physical movement, and no one there physically did it.

I recall another night; my brother had an employee who was in the army before. He operated in the military in a very special and highly skilled 'operations unit' of the military. He was there at the house and worked for my brother. It was a late night, and my brother was away from the house. I was at the house alone. I sensed something was at the door, looked up but didn't see anything. A short while later, the two dogs— The Doberman pinschers—that were outside the door guarding it picked up their heads looked up toward the door and began barking at something that was physically not present. I told him that there was nobody out there, it was a ghost. We all know, ghosts are demons, but I didn't know it then. He grabbed the M16 Assault rifle and went out to investigate. As he made his rounds around the house only to return unfounded, he informed me that nobody was on the property. I told him that it was the ghost. I believe that night he knew what I was telling him was the truth. He just didn't want to think that there was a spiritual realm and these things really take place.

I guess it became known, that I was spiritually sensitive as one of my brother's associates, from a few blocks over, showed up in the middle of a night talking about some similar things taking place at his house. Here was a man that could kill you without any problem at all, but now stood before this kid fearful over something that he physically could not control. I went over with him to check it out and sensed that there was something there. I told it to leave, and it did.

The interesting thing about the many years of sensing this darkness is the massive oppression and depression that I experienced for so many of those years until the age of 31. Yes, that is the age I accepted Jesus Christ as Lord and Savior, but that is coming later in the book.

Another strange part of that period of my life was not being able to have friends come over and spend the night or visit due to the nature of my brother's work as a drug dealer. One afternoon as I arrived home from school, I found a friend of mine Jason from elementary school. He lived in a neighboring town called Atascocita that I previously lived in. He was in my driveway as his brother was purchasing drugs to resell. I recall being in such a state of shock that day that my friend was going down such a terrible path, but I had become so accustomed to this form of life that I shrugged it off and moved on.

Living in a state of depression and not even realizing it, for these years, I didn't even see the damage that was unfolding.

A FAMILY BIRTHDAY

My birthday was approaching soon. My biological father Ron had driven down from Louisiana (where he lived) to celebrate my birthday with my mother and my brother and me.

We made plans to go to Astroworld Amusement Park in Houston. It was an enormous park with roller coaster rides and lots of great attractions. It even had a water park. It was a part of the Six Flags Family.

On June 27th, I was heading to bed excited to wake up the next day to go to Astroworld with my mom, my biological dad Ron, and my brother. I had been waiting for the family being together for very long. It was hard to believe that it was happening.

DREAM WITH A MESSAGE

The most interesting thing happened. That night in my sleep, my grandfather came to me in a vision and told me that he was leaving the earth and that he loved me. It was a very real dream as if I was there with him. I woke up the next morning to see Ron and my mother Cynthia at my bedside. Ron began to tell me, "I've got some bad news to share with you." I said, "Yes, I know, and grandfather passed away. He came and told me last night" To see the look of shock on their faces was interesting, to say the least.

WHERE ARE MY EMOTIONS?

My birthday was off to a strange start. The first was the passing of my grandfather. Our plans were redirected from going to Astroworld that day to an unexpected trip to Amarillo, Texas to "to prepare and attend a funeral." I packed a bag, and my biological father Ron and me went off on a road trip to Amarillo, Texas.

We arrived at my grandmother's house on Lewis Lane in Amarillo, Texas and spent some family time together. The next day, the Pastor from the church came, and we all sat down and had a meeting. I remember feeling weird about the Pastor coming, maybe even a bit condemned, probably due to the things that I've been through and done in life. He began to ask questions about my grandfather to my grandmother and biological father. He wanted to know the details about his life. It shocked me. "Wow! How unknown we are the people who are supposed to be close to us in this place called the church." About an hour later, he wrapped up the details he had written in his pad and departed in a nice friendly way. The ball was rolling.

Our next stop was the funeral home where all the details were put in place. The decision was made, and it was just a matter of waiting for a few days for the burial services to commence. The next night, at my grandmother's house, I was pretty excited actually to have some time with my father. He informed me that he was going to spend some time with an old girlfriend of his from Amarillo. Of course, being the tough boy (externally at least), I nodded my head with a smile and said "Okay." Inside, I was yet once again crushed that a woman had taken priority over me and began to question myself, 'why wasn't I good enough and always seem to take a second seat to every woman, boat, and motorcycle?'

He arrived back at my grandmother's house late that night, and I contemplated, 'Am I going to go to bed or deal with this tonight?' I was entertaining the thoughts of interacting with him and acting like everything was hunky dory. What if he tells me he had sex with her? No surely he will not. As time would have it, he showed back up late that night. I kept the smile on my face and figured that it was just like the rest of my life – broken, chaotic, confused, let down and without purpose or sense. He began to joke around and jab at me with karate moves and open and close stances and so forth. He was apparently trying to smooth it over. He laid his pallet there on the living room floor;

the shock was about to hit. He begins to discuss his night with the lady and the intimacies they had shared together. It's not necessarily something a young man wants to hear when he's always second, third or fourth. It was something a young man, especially a son, should never hear, but it's a part of the brokenness of what the enemy brings in to destroy families. Honestly, at this point, my desire to be with him yet once again went from excited to "I just want to get back to my mom."

That day the funeral couldn't come fast enough, but when it arrived, I was shocked. I had no emotions like other people, who were crying and upset. I was numb. I couldn't find a tear inside. It wasn't because I didn't love my grandfather. I believe that it was just because I dealt with so many losses in my life and brokenness, that I was just flat numb.

RETURN TO RESTORE

One day, my mother informed me that my father Ed was going to return from Midland, Texas from living with his mom and dad and getting back on track with the Lord. He went there to spend some time getting back in a relationship with Jesus Christ. As he arrived back there, we began to reintegrate. He had a lot of changes in him; God was doing great work on and in him. Soon, we found ourselves moving to another place yet again. We didn't have a whole lot of money, but we were able to pull enough together to relocate to an apartment in a village located in Kingwood, Texas. There was a strange excitement in me to come back together and try this family thing again.

I remember the first day we went to look at the apartment. It was a cozy two-bedroom apartment with a vaulted ceiling in the living room. We got there and began to move our stuff in. I thought to myself, "What a lovely place!"

We began to spend our time together, and it seemed a bit different. As we spent the next weeks and months together, things were better, but they were nowhere near perfect. In fact, the range of being close to right was a far distance.

WHERE IS MY FATHER?

My dad Ed moved back out not long after we moved to the new apartment, leaving my mother and me again. My mom had to drive an hour each way to work each day. She worked from 8 am-5 pm. She would drive back home through traffic and arrive at about 6:30 pm, and sometimes even at 7 pm. It drained her, yet she never complained. Throughout my mother's life, she continually took physical and mental beatings. It was the work of the enemy, trying to destroy her as well.

With all this free time, I began to move off in the areas that were becoming a new level of darkness in my life. I began to experiment with a whole new level of very unhealthy sexual ways, with different people. I started to drink a lot and went on to some drugs. At this point, I started taking my mother's car out and joyriding around Kingwood without her knowledge until one day; I got pulled over by the Harris County Pct.4 constables office. I was with my friend Knox. He was a horrible influence in my life and caught up in some very wicked things, and he was out that day with me. The police immediately allowed him to exit the vehicle and leave. When he walked off, I wondered, 'what kind of friend are you?' Later, I got taken to jail, and the car got towed. On the way to the jail in Humble, Texas, the cop began to explain to me that what I was doing was wrong, and the negative impact it could have on my mother and me. I was surprised that he wasn't beating me down. In fact, it was the opposite. He also planted a seed that day that stuck with me for years. I sat in jail that day, and I heard them talking about how they were about to transfer me down to the major jail in downtown. It is the Harris County Jail, and there is nothing pretty or gentle about it. All the bad things that would take place there didn't excite me. Coming from the family where my brother had been to jail many times and hearing his stories, I knew it was the truth. By the grace of God, my mother showed up to the jail to pick me up. I felt so regretful for letting her down, knowing how hard she was working and struggling to keep us on our feet and moving forward. We made it back and got the car back, but nothing else was said or done.

CHAPTER 04: OFF TO THE MANSION

CHAPTER 05

What Is Love

I was an angry and rebellious young man. One thing I learned is, if you don't love yourself or even like yourself, it becomes impossible to get along with other people and to love them. This was pretty much the daily story of my life—living in the state of manic depression, hate, anger, having no hope; now, being very involved in very unhealthy sexual habits, drinking, and drugs.

A lady named Shirley moved in our apartment complex. She had a lot of issues. I began to hang out and spend time with her and her daughter at her apartment in Kingwood. We would drink together and hang out a lot. She had a Volkswagen bug that she would allow me to drive around, and I did. One night, I loaded my friends up in her Volkswagen bug feeling tall and mighty, and we went on a joy ride. We were happy-go-lucky going down a long street through this friendly neighborhood filled with very well-to-do homes. It was called Kings Forest located just behind Kingwood High School. We came around the corner, and there sit a stop sign and not many good options. It was either turn left or right going forward was nothing but trees. We were coming down the street at a high rate of speed. I went to press down on the Volkswagen brakes to stop as we approached the stop sign, but the brakes had gone out. I knew we had to either go right or left because going straight was not a survivable option. We were going to hit the trees, so I took turned the car to a hard left. The car goes up on two wheels and almost flips over. I remember thinking in my head, 'Help me, God.' It came to a stop, fell back to the ground on all four wheels, and we all are just sitting there. I thanked God that night because I knew it was a miracle of God, and God alone, that we weren't flipped over or wrecked into those trees. In fact, the brakes were now working again. Needless to say, I drove us back to my apartment complex very slowly where I returned the car to her and never drove it again.

In that season of time, I was conducting or rather DJ-ing music for the YMCA every Friday night for their dance. Being in such a depressive state all the time, I always wanted to play slow music, and everyone else wanted fast music. I always listened but didn't respond.

WHATS HAPPENING HERE

One Saturday, my biological father, was in town visiting my brother. He was with his wife, Diane. My niece, Reagan Lynn, was crucial to me. Honestly, I can say that she was the only thing I cared for in this world for many years. It was a very depressing time of my life when she was born, and every time I would hold her in my hands I would feel love and peacefulness. Her birth and existence gave me a reason to want to live and move forward. When I came over to my brother's house, he told me that my niece was inside with my dad and his wife, taking a nap. I became outraged and honestly, I felt extremely threatened. I became verbal toward my brother in his driveway which I had never done before because I had feared him all my life. The torment, anger, and rage he'd always put me through in my life put me into a place of submission and of being fearful. That day,

I rose up and told him that it wasn't going to happen.

He punched me in the face and knocked me out. I laid there in the driveway dumbfounded. The hatred I had for my brother rose to another level. I had never felt before and I, honestly, made plans to kill him. These thoughts didn't come to my mind very often, but now it became a priority. Typically, it was me being depressed and not wanting to be on the earth myself, but that day, I started contemplating on removing him from this earth so that he couldn't hurt me or anyone else anymore.

That night, we left his house—and I began to melt down mentally. The lady who had the Volkswagen bug had always spoken of a woman named Janice Costa. She'd always talk about how she would clean Janice's house, how Janice would visit with her, and how sweet and kind she was. She explained how Janice understood her and was helping her. She'd also mention that Janice worked in a facility there in Kingwood, Texas, called Charter Hospital. That night, when I showed up there as a 14-year-old young man who was hitting rock bottom or the bottom of the barrel and finally completely broke open. I sat there talking to the night manager lady at the facility. I told her how I needed to speak to this woman, Janice Costa. She made a phone call and got in touch with Janice at her home and even though Janice Costa didn't know me, she agreed to let me stay there and told me that she would come the next day to speak with me.

A SAFE PLACE

That night, I was placed into a room with another young man who, interestingly enough, had the same last name as I did - Simmons. I began to wonder are we related to each other, why are we in the same room, etc. My mind wandered into the night, but I recall we were told we were going swimming the next day and fell asleep in that thought.

The next day, Janice Costa arrived, and I was called to meet her. I recall not having any fear or strange feelings about the new meeting; in fact, I welcomed it. When I first saw her, I honestly thought that I have just seen an angel. She's so peaceful, loving and kind. I could see that what my friend Shirley had told me was the honest truth. I remember being in a state of confusion in my mind at this point in time. I knew in the depth of my heart that for the first time of my life, I had found somebody who wasn't out to take advantage of me. She was not out to hurt me, abuse me, destroy me, take from me, but rather to help me find my way out of this maze of brokenness and confusion.

The months went ahead, with the goal of getting better, well at least, getting out of there and getting back on my feet. Janice helped me come to an important decision, and I handed the DJ business over to my friend, Andy, who took over the dances and other functions. I made a decision to focus on getting better. I was attending group meetings where we would all sit and discuss our issues and challenges that life had handed us together. I would also have one on one session with Janice who clearly didn't just see herself as a calling from God. Those meetings with Janice were my favorite, and honestly the most productive. They were the most productive because she not only did she have a great ear for listening, but also a dynamic feedback. There were times I avoided dealing with or confronting topics or areas. One day I recall her telling me basically when I was done jerking her chain to let her know, and she would meet with me again. Some may say oh how rude or insensitive, but honestly, it helped me press through and choose to work through to a decision to deal with the issues. She would listen, but unlike others, she didn't look and go "aha"; she would listen and give feedback and help in moving forward.

TIME TO FLY

The time came where I was able to leave Charter for a significant milestone. I had worked hard to get to this day, and it was never a guarantee. I had to aim for the mark and try. In just the right timing, I was released to go on the anticipated trip for my birthday with my grandmother to Hawaii. It was a real blessing as my biological father Ron gave some of his airline miles. My grandmother cashed in a bond for the money we would need for our time there. I remember being on the plane with my grandmother, overlooking the ocean below from 42,000 feet and thinking we are going to have a great time together. I had reservations about returning to the states and trying to love life again. Would it work or once again fail? But hey! I'm on the way to Hawaii; I will deal with that later. When we arrived on the Islands, I was overtaken by the beauty of the water, and the landscape from the air. We touched down and headed to our hotel on the main Island, Honolulu, in our rental car. I asked my grandmother if I could go for exploring the island. Yes, in teenage terms that means go driving. She reluctantly agreed, and I found myself leaving my grandmother in the hotel room while I went driving around in the rental car. I was not out, and up to no good; I believe I was just searching for freedom. I had such desperation for freedom, and I wondered who I am? What group of people are my friends? Why do I exist on this planet? While out driving, I felt sorry about my grandmother being alone at the hotel. So I returned to spend time with her. She expressed to me her concern and at that point, I just couldn't fully understand. Looking back now, it's clear. Again, what is normal? Does it even exist? We chose to stay together, and it felt great! We both agreed the main island was a commercial business type of island so we decided we should move over to Maui, and we did. We made a hop from the Isle of Honolulu and flew over to Maui. We landed on a beautiful tropically vibrant area. There was such excitement! We caught a Taxi to our Hotel which was quite a distance to travel from the airport. We arrived at a large resort with a massive golf course, many story hotel and beautiful bungalows. We settled into our bungalow, and the journey began. We started to have a great time together. We talked, shared, loved, walked on the beach, and ate a lot of pineapple— pineapple on a plate, pineapple in the tea, there was pineapple everywhere. It was a great and glorious time!

A CURIOUS FEELING

I remember meeting a young Polynesian lady who worked in a restaurant there, and for the first time in my life, after all of the years of craziness, loneliness, and just straight confusion, I was finally feeling an emotion towards her that was not of a sexual nature. It was the kind of feeling accepted and understood. As her shift was ending, I walked her to the front where we talked until her ride arrived. She walked away waving and saying goodbye as she got into the car and left. I wanted to believe that I would see her again, but I knew my grandmother Doris's and my time was nearing the completion of our trip there, and we would soon depart back to the states.

CHAPTER 06

THE ✘ MIRACLE CHILD

Where Am I Going?

WHERE IS THE ROAD GOING?

As we came back to the states, the discussion came up about me moving in with my biological father, Ron in Shreveport, Louisiana. He was currently living with another friend but had found an apartment complex up the road to move in. After a lot of thought, I agreed and hoped that this time would be different. So he showed up in Houston, Texas with a trailer being pulled by an old Oldsmobile car. We loaded my stuff up in a car my brother had gotten for me from a junkyard as a project car while I was in the Charter facility. I remember looking at the trailer that day with all the stuff in it and wished for a new start. Honestly, I still felt very helpless, and completely uncertain. We drove off and headed to Shreveport, Louisiana, where I would find my new home. At this point, I was 15 years old. I recall getting settled in, and everything would seem workable there during the day. However, the night would come, and I would get lonely. I hit rock bottom because hopelessness would hit. The voices and thoughts asked, "Why am I even trying? This isn't going to work!" But yet, I would give Janice a call, and she would talk through things with me, which was a real blessing from God. I can honestly say that if God would not have had

Janice there in my life, it's very likely that I wouldn't be here now writing this book.

LIVING ON A FAULTLINE

As time moved on, we made another shift to New Madrid, Missouri. My father had been offered a job there, working for a building company that manufactured concrete cellular, telephone, and equipment buildings. It was a small town of 3,204 people, and it seemed fascinating when we made our journey up there. As we were entering into this little town people were waving. It was a shock. I began to find a little hope. I started attending school there and enjoying the small town. My biological father Ron and I lived in a small two-bedroom apartment that we called home. It was nice!

A SHOCKING RIDE TO LOVE

One day, I was driving my fixed up a project car to wash it at the car wash. This was a Toyota Celica that was broken down and my biological father Ron, and I had worked on. We got the car up and running. As I was driving to the car wash, a car rapidly came up behind me, honking its horn. I inwardly was in a state of shock and anxiety. The car pulled up next to me, and there was a young lady in the passenger seat of the car and another woman who was her mother, Diane. The other woman looked familiar, so I rolled down the window, and they began to say "Hi!" They were very friendly. I breathed a sigh of relief but wondered if everybody was so aggressive in that town. She said, "I don't know if you remember me, but I work at the KonTech office where your dad works at." And then it hit me, "Yes, I remember you." And she said, "I wanted to introduce you to my daughter," and she introduced me to her daughter. Her name was Julie. Me and Diane's daughter Julie began to take an interest in each other and started dating. She was probably one of my first girlfriends that I had come close to in my adolescence age. However, there was another love of my life in elementary school named April. That relationship is the one I will always hold near and dear to my heart. Coming back to Julie, I allowed her into the deeper part of my heart. With anything in life, if it is not directed by the Holy Spirit of God, it will fail, or you will fight to control it to your death.

THE PARTY PALACE

In the midst of this, I started a little teenage dance club, and video game hangout called the *Party Palace*. It was an excellent gathering spot for the small-town people of New Madrid, Lilbourn, and other surrounding towns to come together, especially from The New Madrid Country High School (The Eagles). However, I didn't take into account many considerations; in fact, I didn't even have a business plan. The location was not a good one. The other issue was that on the Main Street in the middle of our small town, there was another get-together spot that got their attention. The season was short for *Party Palace,* but a fun one.

THEN THERE WAS SCHOOL

When we moved to New Madrid, we arrived out of the regular semester and were coming in late to sign me up at The New Madrid County High School. They were able to put me into a program called 'construction trades.' The instructor, a very muscular and authoritative man like a lumberjack, agreed to let me in as he was made aware of my challenges and knew my history. His name was Mr. Townley. It was great! Each afternoon, we would go in and get our tools together and occasionally have a team meeting. We got on the bus and traveled to our worksite where we built a house from the foundation to completion. Mr. Townley was a patient but straight man. He was a man who believed in me and encouraged me. I thank God for this man. He was another person God had put on my path of coming out of rejection and destruction. His impact on me and my life would reflect in my mentoring and fathering young people in the later years of my life.

THE REFEREE CALLS A FOUL

The referee called a foul as I was dating my girlfriend Julie and my father started to date her mother, Diane. In the midst of this, Julie decided to leave me and found another man. It broke me up. I was back to that place of rejection again— "What did I do wrong? Why was I not good enough?"— When the reality was that, she was just moving on.

ANOTHER CURVE BALL

Well, the announcement wasn't far off. My biological father Ron announced to me that he was getting married to Diane. That was my ex-girlfriend's mother. I wasn't happy about it and, to be honest with you, I was angry. Unknown feelings of uncertainty, rejection, rebellion, and so much more arose in me. I remember the day it came around to them getting married and going to this small church in Lilbourn, and I didn't want to be involved or even be there. At the same time, I did not desire to hurt anyone either. I questioned myself that day, "Why am I feeling this way toward this lady? She seems nice, and she had never done anything bad to me" when the reality was that it was just the rejection I received through all the years from all the other women my dad had put before me.

THE FAMILY KNOT

They tied the knot, and the next step was that everybody moved into one house, under one roof. A doublewide trailer had been purchased, put on a piece of land and we decided to make the best of it. We all moved in, and my and my stepmother Diane's relationship was just getting started.

One day in the kitchen I was assisting her in making spaghetti and meatballs. We were the only ones there, and she asked me if I could drain the spaghetti noodles and water. Outwardly, I wanted to be strong and show her and everyone that I didn't need her, but inwardly I didn't want to be enemies. I just wanted to be loved again. Honestly, I just did not want to get hurt again. I agreed and went to pour the water through a strainer into the sink. As I poured the spaghetti out into the strainer, it spilled into the sink directly. I immediately felt the feeling of failing and being a failure rising in me once again. I will never forget what followed. She looked at me with such a sense of love and acceptance. The love and peace she showed me that day cracked a door open. She began to laugh and came over and just scooped it back in the pan after a little washing. Diane smiled and said that no one will ever know what happened there, and we fixed it! I had found a new friendship that made a huge turn in our relationship. We were in a great direction.

BACK TO HOUSTON

I returned to Houston to share an apartment with my brother Barrett near the Compaq Center, which was the home of the Houston Rockets. It was an enjoyable time of my continued mixed emotions. I'll tell you, a life without Jesus is just straight torment! I met a girl at these apartments named Mary that I liked tremendously, but yet again I ran from another relationship out of fear and confusion.

DEEPER DARKNESS

As the years progressed, I found myself caught up in even greater levels of darkness. I was living a life of darkness strangely trying to find love in the wrong place. The truth is love is only found in Jesus Christ. Why it took me so many years to surrender and accept His perfect love, often blows my mind.

DEMONIC SEX

As the years progressed in this life of dysfunction and darkness, I found myself living in Garden Villas in South Houston. I got into a sexual encounter one night with a vampire. It was the strangest night of demonic darkness I have ever experienced. As we were engaged in these immoral acts, suddenly, it ceased. I looked out the windows and clearly saw the street light with clear visibility. It transformed into a total fog in about 30 seconds. The atmosphere of the room was shifted as well. The presence of evil increased to a whole other level.

JEZEBEL MANIFESTS

As the years continued flowing forth, I was now in a position of living with a family. It was a family of four- the father who was a Mason, the mother who raised horses and had a high Jezebel spirit, and two children one who were always plagued with a spirit of infirmity. The mother took a liking to me and began to move in on me. I had no interest, but she didn't understand that signal. She began to stalk me at my apartment in

Pasadena, and go on about abandoning her family and mainly her. It was getting very out of control when, one evening, it finally came to an abrupt end. I had no idea at that time about the differing places of darkness in our lives, but they are real. I was working for an ambulance in Pasadena, Texas when she arrived and began to beat on the door of the building making threats to my life. She got in her truck and started to squeal the tires. I had to call the police to come and remove her.

FREEDOM OR DESTRUCTION

Everyone says that they dislike drama and yet continue the same lifestyle day in and day out- Drinking, smoking, sex, drugs, etc. The reality is that our supposed independence is masked to a reality of bondage as Satan's tools. We must understand that the senses are the gates, and what comes in them can strengthen our faith in the Lord or to destroy us. Yes, we must surrender to Christ Jesus, but He has given us free will and that makes it our decision!

The bible does say this about an unstable man "*he is* a double-minded man, unstable in all his ways. Let the lowly brother glory in his exaltation, but the rich in his humiliation, because as a flower of the field he will pass away." James 1:8-10

MOVING ON UP

I began to look for different work than Emergency medical services (the ambulance) as my friend Anthony had informed me that his father had hired him in computers. It made sense to me as I was a BBS guy. For those of you that don't know what that is, it stands for Bulletin Board System. It was a dial-up through the telephone line system yes pre-fast internet. I went to many headhunter services and many interviews. I walked in with confidence for many of the interviews and finally landed a temporary which turned into a full-time job position at Energy Ventures Incorporated. I started as a PC technician and worked my way up to overseeing the networks and operations at three facilities, one of which was a fresh take over called Grant Prideco in Navasota, Texas. The folks there were not too friendly, as I was from corporate and they were not used to being taken care of. As I invested my time there and began to assign computers to the right resources to the right departments in an attempt to get people to a greater level of functionality, they began to warm up to me. The interesting thing was that the corporate began to see what I was doing and eventually gave me an unlimited budget for the facility. It felt like a great accomplishment in my life, but here comes the problem- The love of money. I watched as some of the network engineers pulled the I am not getting enough money game and advised they would leave without a raise. Well, they would continuously give them raises. So, one day, I marched right in and gave it a try, and it worked. I went from making $48,000 a year to nearly $90,000 a year. They were providing me a company car, gas, and all the goodies as well. The hunger for money just increased, and I was on a roller coaster ride. I went in one

morning and told them that I needed more money or I was going to move to Baker Hughes Information Technologies. They said they would discuss it, but little did I know that the roller coaster was about to derail. I was half way to the Navasota facility, and I received a phone call advising to come back to corporate. I said that I would work the full day, but I was barred from the building. I returned to find my resignation was effective immediately with two weeks paid. I called my head hunter Laura Guzzetta and told her that I would take the Baker Hughes job. When I arrived at the Baker Hughes facility, I immediately found out I would not be enjoying this job as my freedom was gone. I stayed there for a few weeks and said no more! After that, she found me a new position at Basis Petroleum, which was acquired shortly after that by Valero Refining group. I enjoyed this job and was a network administrator on the Novell platform, desktop analyst, and a Meridian phone system administrator. I had great freedom at this job and found that I worked well with freedom. An opportunity arose with a company called VanCom Systems, Inc. VanCom was a systems integration company and was run by a man named Don Vann. Don was a Christian man who would passively share Jesus Christ with me and planted some good seeds. One day, I and Edwin, who was another employee, walked into an office meeting and Don stated that we would no longer have a job. He was shutting the company down as his wife, Lisa, did not like his long hours at the office. He gave us two weeks pay, but now the awesome job that I had let go off at Valero Refinery was history. So I had no other choice but to start my company called SimCom / Network Resolutions. I worked my business for several years and one day had a new client account opened with Cynthia Watts, who was an attorney. I was requested to make a service call to her home office and responded to fix her computer. As I was going through her computer, I noticed a file named Harold Price. I asked myself, 'could this be the same man?' So I asked Cynthia Watts if this man was the man in question and she confirmed it was, in fact, him. I asked her to please give him my contact information, and she agreed. Not long after my service call, I received a phone call from Harold, and he invited me to lunch. We met over lunch at Bennigans Restaurant, and he shared a new company he was opening called Titanic, which provided full range I.T. Service. He then made an offer to purchase my business and have me come over as the vice president and general manager of the company. I graciously refused his offer and made my way back to my office near the George Bush Intercontinental Airport in North Houston, Texas. As the days went forward, I reflected on his offer and some of the brick walls I was facing in the current business model of SimCom Network Resolutions. One afternoon, I made a call to Harold and asked if the offer was still on the table and Harold said that it was. My request was that all my employees be brought over as well and he agreed. Titanis was a great experience that brought me the opportunity to open business with many companies, but the one that would be the bad fruit on the tree would me the music industry. A large part of my business had become offering touring productions and fan clubs solutions which put me on the 2003 MTV TRL Tour with Destiny's Child, Nelly, and much more. In this process, I almost married the fan club president Jennette. Back at Titanis offices, I was having a conflict with a man that was brought in later in the game named Mike. Mike and I clashed and had differing visions. People that had been loyal to Harold were being axed from their jobs right and left, and I came to the final decision. I'm done! I went back to operating my company, and this is when my best friend Mikey and my father Ed passed away.

Things began to come to a new level of low. I started drinking again and became very involved in destructive acts in my life and making poor choices. I was having many sexual relations, drinking, and incredibly depressed.

It was 2004, and it had been a rough year.

What I am referring to was 18 months before my father Ed was in the Methodist Hospital undergoing yet another surgery in the aorta of his heart. As my dad was taken into the pre-operative room, he and I and sat in the small hallway alone. He looked up at me and said, son, if I do not return from the operating room alive I am at peace. I was shocked and refused to accept what he was saying to me. I just responded dad you will be ok! The hours began to tick away, and they became prolonged until Dr. Zimmerman came out and spoke to me. I was the one in the family with the medical understanding and had been with my father to nearly every doctor appointment he had gone to. After a prolonged surgery, Dr. Zimmerman said that they could not close him that night. My dad Ed's blood would not clot due to the extensive liver damage in his body. I asked, "what exactly does that mean?" Dr. Zimmerman said, "tomorrow morning it will either be life or death." I had heard it so many times from different doctors and surgeons in my dad's life, but this time something was different. I was scared! I told our family of the report. My mother, Aunt Tina, step sister Mellissa, Grandmother Mimi, and other family members were there. We made our way across the street to the Hotel and went up to Mimi's room. The family was across the room praying, and I sat on the other side of the room angry with God in my heart. I asked him 'why would you do this to my father?' I had no clue of God's goodness at that point.

WALK WITH ME

After they were done praying my sister Mellissa approached me with love. She asked if I would escort her to her room, and I agreed. It was a quiet walk to her room. We arrived at her door, and she unlocked and opened it. She asked me if I would come in for a few minutes. As I entered her room, being quiet as her husband and son were asleep, she began to talk with me. If there was someone on earth who could get through and speak to me, I had given her that place for some reason. She proceeded to ask me what my problem with God was. As she asked me that I honestly wondered 'what is my problem with God?' She said something to me that would come to be a huge part of my surrender to God. She said, "You need to get right with God!" She hugged me, and I left feeling dumbfounded. If anyone else had said that to me, I probably would have gone off on them, but my sister had that place in my life.

CHAPTER 07

THE MIRACLE CHILD

A Plea Deal With God

As I arrived home at 3:30 AM that morning I went straight to my office. I sat in my chair and thought 'how does this work? How do you talk to God?' I was desperate for my dad's life. There was so much we still had not done, still had not talked about. This cannot happen now! That's when I called out to God and had a conversation with Him about the situation with my dad. I said to God "If you give my dad more time, I will give you my life." I felt peace after that and headed back to the Methodist Hospital. As I arrived, it was approaching 6 AM. They were to start the surgery soon, and here comes Dr. Reardon through the double doors. I went to meet him halfway expecting to hear that they were about to initiate the surgery. Instead, he reported a miracle. Yes, Dr. Reardon said "we went in earlier, and were able to close him fine.' I immediately knew that God had come though and brought my dad a miracle. I cannot describe the level of thankfulness to the Lord!

GREAT TIME TOGETHER

In our days ahead, we utilized the time together. I took every opportunity to fill in the holes of our relationship. The thoughts of losing my father Ed in the hospital were thoughts that never departed my mind. I recall thinking he could die. We will never be able to fill in the holes, but we saw that God was so gracious that He gave us this time to complete what had been started. We did just that, and I was so thankful.

THE FINAL ROUND

A year later, my father, Ed was again admitted to the Methodist Hospital. It seemed like another round in the boxing ring. I was beside my dad daily, as I had always been for the many years before. They did an MRI of his body, and the doctor asked me to sit down with him to go over the results. He began to show the slices of the lung through the MRI imagery computer, and there was a large mass in the center of the left lung. My heart sank, but I remembered the many victories we have had before. I knew we would have them again... right? I went into my father's hospital room, and we talked about the procedure. He agreed to go ahead with it- a test was done on his lung. I went down to the cafeteria and received a phone call a short time later saying that they could not complete the lung biopsy, an d he had gone into respiratory arrest. I rushed back upstairs and waited for my father to be returned to his room in the ICU. He returned and I spent time there with him comforting him.

I'M READY TO GO HOME SON

As we talked about the challenges he had experienced with the respiratory arrest, I encouraged him and said that we could reschedule it, and it would work this time. He asked me to sit down, and I sat at the edge of his hospital bed. He said to me, "Son, I need to talk to you about something important." I said "okay, " and he said, "I am ready to go home now." I said, "We just need to finish these tests, and it won't be long before we are out of here." My father said, "No. I am ready to go home. Willing to go to Heaven to be with Jesus and God. I came back and did what He told me to do. I'm ready to go home now." I was totally dumbfounded and completely lost at this point. I kept thinking that this cannot be over. We have always kept going, always fought and won. I said to my father "Ok I understand" and had to escape. I kept it together as I did not want to discourage him. I departed to my car in the parking garage fighting back the tears and confusion. I arrived at my car and had a complete meltdown. I cried like I don't think I had cried before. My heart was broken and lost. I couldn't lose my father... This couldn't be happening, but it was...

We made arrangements for him to come home in hospice. He was coming home to spend his final days here. Things began shifting as people were delivering hospital beds to his apartment overlooking downtown, and he arrived home.

It was a difficult time, as he began to sleep more and more, until one day he was confined to a chair with his jaw open, having difficulty in breathing, and much more.

TO LIVE OR TO DIE... THIS IS MY CONFUSION

As he was experiencing respiratory difficulty, I called the hospice center and requested them that they needed to send the nurse out immediately. He was in respiratory distress, and we needed to fix this now before he entered respiratory and cardiac arrest. My father was dying. They were kindly telling me that the nurse would come out tomorrow, and I went ballistic on them screaming and cursing. He could not die; this could not be happening. They agreed to send a nurse, and she arrived at about 2:45 AM. I began to urge her that we needed to take an immediate action to prevent my father from dying. If we didn't fix this respiratory issue, he would die. She calmly asked me to sit down on the couch and began to explain the process to me. She was sent by the God. After explaining, she asked if she could pray for my mother and me, and we agreed. She then began to share Jesus with us. Those seeds took ground.

A DECISION THAT ALMOST KILLED ME

The hospice nurse addressed my concern with my father's respiratory issues and his discomfort. She advised it was the time to administer Haldol and morphine to him to deal with the pain. I knew that once we did, there was no turning back. But the pain he was in was extreme. The decisions for his medical had always been primarily up to me as I had gotten a little older. I agreed reluctantly, and she administered the medicines.

He began just to sit in the family chair in the living room and could not open his eyes, and he could barely shut his mouth as his jaw had locked open. He would try to tell my mother to pick him up and walk him around the living room, but his weight was difficult. It seemed he didn't want to stop trying.

I could not stand seeing him like this. It was breaking me inside. That night, I asked my mother if we should pray and ask God to take him home. She agreed that we should. I grabbed his Bible and ended up at Psalm 98, 99, 100, and 101. I read this out loud to God and my father honestly having no clue at all about what I was doing, but I was just trusting that God was in control.

READING PSALM 98, 99, and 100

PSALM 98

A Song of Praise to the Lord for His Salvation and Judgment

Oh, sing to the Lord a new song!
For He has done marvelous things;
His right hand and His holy arm have gained Him the victory.

The Lord has made known His salvation;

His righteousness He has revealed in the sight of the nations.

He has remembered His mercy and His faithfulness to the house of Israel;

All the ends of the earth have seen the salvation of our God.

Shout joyfully to the Lord, all the earth;

Break forth in song, rejoice, and sing praises.

Sing to the Lord with the harp,

With the harp and the sound of a psalm,

With trumpets and the sound of a horn;

Shout joyfully before the Lord, the King.

Let the sea roar, and all its fullness,

The world and those who dwell in it;

Let the rivers clap their hands;

Let the hills be joyful together before the Lord,

For He is coming to judge the earth.

With righteousness, He shall judge the world,

And the peoples with equity.

PSALM 99
Praise to the Lord for His Holiness

The Lord reigns;

Let the peoples tremble!

He dwells between the cherubim;

Let the earth be moved!

The Lord is great in Zion,

And He is high above all the peoples.

Let them praise Your great and awesome name—

He is holy.

The King's strength also loves justice;

You have established equity;

You have executed justice and righteousness in Jacob.
Exalt the Lord our God,
And worship at His footstool—
He is holy.
Moses and Aaron were among His priests,
And Samuel was among those who called upon His name;
They called upon the Lord, and He answered them.
He spoke to them in the cloudy pillar;
They kept His testimonies and the ordinance He gave them.
You answered them, O Lord our God;
You were to them God-Who-Forgives,
Though You took vengeance on their deeds.
Exalt the Lord our God,
And worship at His holy hill;
For the Lord our God is holy.

Psalm 100
A Psalm of Thanksgiving.

Make a joyful shout to the Lord, all you lands!
Serve the Lord with gladness;
Come before His presence with singing.
Know that the Lord, He is God;
It is He who has made us, and not we ourselves;
We are His people and the sheep of His pasture.
Enter into His gates with thanksgiving,
And into His courts with praise.
Be thankful to Him, and bless His name.
For the Lord is good;
His mercy is everlasting,
And His truth endures to all generations.

RELEASE AND PRAYER

After reading the bible as I sat on the left side of my father, and my mother sat on the floor. I suggested we should tell dad that it was okay to leave now and go home to be with the Lord. We should pray, and ask God to receive him. My mother agreed, and we did.

I THINK HE HAS DIED

As I was asleep on the couch in the living room by my father, my mother woke me at 2:30 AM and told me, "Brent I believe that he has passed away." I arose from the couch and went over to check my father's pulse and respirations. He had no pulse or respirations and had passed on to be with the Lord in Glory.

I told my mother that I was going to get some work done. I called Chad in who worked for me in my computer company Simcom I.T. Solutions and informed him what had happened and that we were going to work. He tried to encourage me to take some time off, but I was running again. I needed to be busy, so we headed off to a law firm that was a client in downtown. The funeral home came to pick my father up. Honestly, I could not be there at that time.

The thoughts began to plague me day in and day out that I had killed my father by allowing the nurse to administer the Haldol and Morphine. The thoughts that I murdered my dad, and my best friend Mikey passing away just six months earlier were taking a path to a downward spiral. This would drive me to a deeper low to hit bottom.

AN INDEPENDENCE TO REMEMBER

I was working on my business that was failing. I could not

keep my head above the water due to depression and a lack of hope. On July 4th, 2004, I was working on the 9th floor in my small computer information technologies business office located in the Houston House High Rise building in downtown Houston. I began to hear a fire alarm sounding while I was there with a friend. Having a history of firefighting, I was well aware of the danger of high-rise building fires. They are amongst the most dangerous ones, and there was extreme potential for massive loss of life. As I exited my office on the 9th floor on a mission to save lives, I never took my own into consideration. I had no bunker gear, breathing apparatus, or radio lifeline. Honestly, it never crossed my mind because, at that point in life, my life did not matter to me. I entered the stairwell to find it filled back to back with people going down the stairs in a rapid and somewhat frantic state. I asked 'where is the fire?' Many gave me the deer in the headlights look and couldn't respond. Finally, a lady replied that it was on the 12th floor. I began going against the people, ascending the stairs to the 12th floor to evacuate any victims that may have been there. As I arrived on the 12th floor, I checked the door and found extreme heat. I entered the door, and I found the hallway filled with smoke, and a door directly across the hall with heavy fire coming through. I grabbed a house hand line and attempted to knock the fire down, but quickly determined that the hand line was making no impact. I was low on the floor and making my way down the hallway to knock on the doors and explain the people out to safety. All were clear from the 12th floor, and I made my way from the floor to the stairwell. As I went down the stairs feeling light headed, I made it to the ground floor to be met by Houston Fire Department paramedics approaching me with concern. They began to attempt treating me, and I insisted them to help the others first. One of the medics said that the others are okay because of your actions.

I then accepted, and they began to treat me for smoke inhalation with oxygen and a heart monitor. My body did not like the poisoning of the smoke, and I was experiencing heart arrhythmias, and respiratory distress. The medics were encouraging me to go to the hospital, and I continually denied transport. They told me that there was a high possibility of death, and I responded that I was previously a medic and was aware of the risks. The Fire Department shift commander came over while I was lying on the stretcher and started debriefing me on what had taken place. I told the shift commander of the events, and he said to me "your rapid intervention saved hundreds of lives today. Great job!" He thanked me and advised me that he was putting me in to receive a key to the city of Houston for the courageous act done there. I made a choice not to go and receive the key to the city as I had thoughts of having failed so many times, and finally doing something that helped people to survive. I didn't feel I deserved the key at that point in life. The paramedics continued to insist that I go to the hospital to get checked out as I had very red lips and shortness of breath which was a sign of carbon monoxide poisoning and respiratory failure. So I finally agreed to go with them. At the hospital, people began to ask me if I was the one who rescued the people from the building. I remember thinking that it was not a big deal and anyone could do it. Right? Not long after that, I was feeling very overwhelmed and told the doctors that I needed to leave. They refused to let me leave due to the level of poison in blood from the smoke, so I left against medical advice and made my way to Pasadena where I walked to my friend's home as if nothing had happened. They asked, 'Are you ok? We've been trying to call you?' I said "Yes, I am fine. Why?" They said 'You are all over the news, the high-rise fire...' I didn't want to discuss it. I was just glad that it was over and nobody got hurt. Well, except me, but as usual I was running from everybody, everything and myself.

PART III
Surrender

CHAPTER 08

Rock Bottom

HOME ALONE

Portions of the Houston House high rise were opened for residents to re-enter after the fire. A few floors remained under reconstruction. I came back home to find myself finally hitting rock bottom. I found myself sitting there, looking over the city from the 23rd floor. It was such a beautiful view. The thoughts of my two crutches being gone were killing me. I no longer had anyone to hold me up. You wonder 'Richard, what crutches are you referring to?' My two crutches were my father, Ed Cox and my best friend, Mikey. Mikey was murdered in the military, and six months later my dad Ed passed away. In my world at that point, I had zero hope. We will just say that attempts to leave early failed, and I was angry at God. As I sat there not wanting to exist anymore, I heard the voice of God say to me "You gave me your life."

A VOICE FROM THE PAST

On July 12, 2004, I listened to a knock on my door. I was surprised as usually the security downstairs calls and informs me that guests are here to visit. I opened the door to find a friend from the past- Oscar. He didn't look like the friend I knew from the past. You ask why? Well, good question. In earlier years, he was a gang member that sold crack and cocaine on the streets of Houston. He came from a fatherless home and was experiencing a lot of rejection. As I stood there looking at the change in his appearance, I saw a young man that no longer had a gold grill in his mouth and he no longer had a gang flag hanging from his back pocket. He was cleaned up and was looking sharp. He was wearing a Nautica shirt, tan pants, and polo boots. He asked me "Are you going to invite me in?" and I said "yes, of course." He came in, and we sat in the living room and talked for a while. The unspoken question was what had happened. He opened up and began to tell me that he was married, had a child and was going to the church. I was shocked and dumbfounded, to say the least. I knew that the question was coming, but I just did not know when. He said that I should go to church with him and his wife tomorrow. I was internally going *umm...* Well, I agreed to go, thinking he was so much crazier than I ever was; and in those days I was pretty stupid. I said to myself "how am I going to tell him no..." I called my mother and a few close friends that night and asked them to join me on a visit to the church the following day. Most of them thought that I had lost my mind, and honestly, I thought the same as well.

OFF TO CHURCH WE GO

The next morning we all headed off to the Lakewood Church in Houston, Texas. It was July 14th, and I was doing everything I could to skip the message and get to the end of the service already; to move on with my perfectly crappy life, I had been living for so many years. However, as Joel was delivering the message, I found myself catching keywords that were aimed towards me, clearly by the God. I began to question "Is this man speaking to me? How? He doesn't know me. Did my friend call him and tell him about my life?" So many questions... But I came to figure this out that whatever it was, this man was speaking to me and it was on point. I realized this was much more than anyone could figure out or organize especially with me sitting in the upper seat of the church. I found myself intently listening to the message and receiving the fullness of it.

I WANT THIS JESUS

At the end of the message, they made a call to accept Jesus Christ as Lord and Savior. I decided that I want to know this Jesus and make Him Lord over my life. As I tried to stand up, I was shocked that I was bound there in my seat. I literally could not move a muscle in my body or speak. I was demonized. I was scared, and I wondered how could that be, I was in a church. The enemy is not allowed here. Oh, what things I had to learn. In my mind, I said to the Lord God, "Please help me," and He freed me. I felt the muscle in my right leg twitch and then I was assisted by the angels to rise. As I was standing, I realized that the knots and the big bumps in my back were no longer there. They were all gone. My neck muscles were completely free as well. Wow, this was a feeling I had never known. The peace I felt at that point was incredible.

Having a fresh start, I began going to church every time the doors were open. I hungered for truth and the new freedom that, I knew, had to be in Christ. I always enjoyed worshipping, and it was so freeing that I could always feel His presence and his touch. You know, the feeling that has freedom and love to it. WOW, how I love His touch! Day in and day out, I would yearn for the church to open the doors so I could go again. I knew how messed up I was, and how I needed change. I yearned to have a personal relationship with some brothers but had no friends that knew God. That is one of the problems with the MegaChurch movement. It is just too vast and unconnected. I started praying and asking God to connect me.

MEET THIS MAN

As I went on a trip to Tennessee, He revealed to me that when I returned, I would meet a brother. I didn't know his name, but I had seen an image of him in a vision. I knew it was in the main lobby area across the bookstore. I returned and waited, hoping, but not seeing anyone that looked like him. I knew in the depth of my heart that I had seen and I believed. At that moment, a young man walked up. He was tall, thin and wearing a suit. He just stood there. I was so excited, and I knew that this was him. I approached him, and out of nowhere, we just hit it off. I shared my story with him of God showing me to meet him there. His name was Brandon, and he was a prayer partner. He had to go to pre-service prayer pretty soon but asked me if I knew the Holy Spirit. I said no, but I want to know Him. Brandon took me to the library and bought me a small book by John Osteen about coming to know the Holy Spirit. Brandon asked me to read the book and wrote his number on the back of the book. He said to call him after I had read it, as he rushed off for the pre-service prayer. I read the book over the next day, and I did give him that call! I came to know a group of brothers that I met at the Church-Brandon, Lucio, and Jorge. Lucio was a prophet from Mexico, and he was someone I had never seen before. Lucio invited me to attend a gathering at his apartment, and I felt moved to participate. I began to attend the meetings at his apartment in Houston where we would pray and seek God. He would prophesize what the Lord was saying, and sowed into my life. He was a very straight but honest man. What you saw was what you got. He was no man pleaser! A true prophet in every sense. Lucio began helping me walk out a challenging walk with God and led me through deliverance. He did not make it easy, but it was so very real. Lucio had such a sincere heart from God and would stop at nothing to share the fullness. Sometimes, I rebelled against Lucio out of a feeling of rejection from the past, but he kept going forward. That always impressed me and set right within me. Lucio was the real deal, and I thank God for his steadfast love that I didn't exactly understand. I was a new pup dealing with a man of extreme authority, a true prophet of God.

DEVIL GO IN JESUS NAME

One evening we agreed to set a meeting for my deliverance from lust and rejection. He wanted to do this deliverance at the University of Houston in Downtown Houston, and hungry for freedom, I agreed. We met on the upper floor and went through my deliverance in the hallway. It may not always be pretty or cute, but if you seriously want your freedom you don't care where, when, how, or anything else!

LORD USE ME

The hurricane came through and had a direct impact on New Orleans, Louisiana and caused major devastation. The hurricane was named Katrina, and it sent people homeless across the United States. We had many arrive here in Houston, and Lucio had arranged for us to go and do prayer counseling. We arrived at the Astrodome and Astro Hall area. We went on with praying as a team for many people. As we entered the Astro Hall, Lucio was talking with a young lady who wanted an Old Testament

Bible, but Lucio had only new testaments. He was convincing her that she needed the truth of Jesus and grace. Out of the right corner of my eye and in my spiritual man, I sensed something. As I looked, I saw a Red Cross person way across the room coming toward us. This person was far across the room, but I knew that person was coming for us...

CHAPTER 09

THE MIRACLE CHILD

A Game Changer

MEDICAL SKILLS OR MIRACLES TO PREVAIL?

Minutes later a person came to us and asked, "Do any of you have medical skills?" I previously worked for the ambulance as an emergency medical technician, so I responded with a yes. Brandon and I headed over to the other side of the hall and saw a lady who had been paralyzed since Louisiana and was now lying on a cot here. Many people accompanying her gave testimony of her not having any movement from New Orleans to where she lay now. I knelt down and asked her a few questions medically and confirmed that she had no movement in her extremities. I stood up and told Brandon that we would go and get her on a triage list for help.

ARE YOU GOING TO PRAY?

As I turned around to walk away, I heard a voice speak to me. He said, "Are you going to pray for her?" I was shocked! I turned around and told my friend Brandon that we must pray for her. So we knelt down and prayed for her. She began to move a little to the right and left and began to scream and stand up. People started running toward us, and I thought we were about to get trampled or beaten. These people were running at us in response to what Jesus had just done for her. He took a completely paralyzed person and totally healed her. He did it right there on the spot. He did not do it through the guy who had a Ph.D., MD or any of that; but the man who was humbly kneeling down saying "Lord, use me to heal the sick, to raise the dead," and that, the Lord did! It was not the guy leading the group. No, it was the guy that just came hoping to be part of how Jesus was healing and restoring the broken and homeless. To be honest, I was in total shock and could not believe it myself. I know healing was real as I had seen it so many times with my father Ed, but wow, in the middle of an Astro Hall in Houston, Texas, with no special skills or crazy deep prayers, etc. Just the prayer from a heart to see someone restored. Knowing that I could not heal her, but He could. In fact, He did and did it through me.

A GAME CHANGER

That day was a game changer for me. I realized God wanted to use me as a part of His team, and my past didn't disqualify me from being used for His purposes and His Glory. I ask you how great our God is?

The chaos and confusion were breaking out; people were robbing stores around us, and yet here Jesus was healing and delivering people from significant infirmities that no man or hospital could do immediately or in that setting. He healed her on the spot! That is the God we serve!

We can place no limits or boundaries on Him. We must surrender our all to him and choose to trust Him as the Healer - The Chief Physician. We cannot heal a flea on a dog's back, but oh Jesus can heal anyone or anything. No limits or boundaries exist with Him. Call out today for your healing. He is the healer and deliverer. ....God is our refuge and strength, a very present help in trouble. (Psalms 46:1 NKJV)

PRISON MINISTRY

One day, I made a service call to help my brother at his office park with some telephone service issues with a new renter. I went out to fix the problem and met a mighty woman of God. Her name was Ms. Helen. I saw a Footprints poem on the wall and a cross in her office. I complimented her, and we began to talk about the Lord's goodness. She invited me to go and do prison ministry, but honestly, that terrified me. I finally agreed that if she could make it happen for the next day, I would go with her. I believed it would not be possible due to all the restrictions and paperwork. Well 10 minutes later, she called, and the warden had approved it. That began a season of prison ministry at the Plane state prison in Dayton, Texas. God showed up in powerful ways there.

HONDURAS MISSION INITIAL

Next, God opened doors to go to the Honduras Thanksgiving of 2006. We traveled to the town of La Ceiba, Honduras, where I began ministering the children in a Boy's home called the Children of the Light. My ministry to Honduras has since spread to Central America as a whole.

While there, the Lord brought two boys to me as sons. Their names were Mario and Marco. They had lived a very difficult and challenging life, but I believe God had a greater plan for them both. They will, one day, enter that fullness in Jesus name.

CHAPTER 09: A GAME CHANGER

CHAPTER 10

THE MIRACLE CHILD

A New Level of Faith

It was 2008, a new time of really stepping out in faith; sensing the Lord in a new way was arising. I guess you can call it reckless faith, reckless abandonment to the Lord. I was in such a place of wanting more of God. I knew there was more and I wanted more. It wasn't an option, and I had to have more. I was so very desperate! My cry was "Lord; I'm desperate. I've got to have more. There was more of you, but I knew that was requiring less of me." That's how it works—more of Him and less of us.

MY PRAYER FOR YOU

My prayer, as you continue to hear my story in this book, is that you will call out to the Holy Spirit and ask for your double portion. That you will look at 1st Kings chapter 19 and read it and see that it's essential that we leave things behind us.   To go forward with the Lord, you've got to leave things behind you.

As you've read in this book so far, there are a lot of things, I've gone through in my life and so many things that I have not written yet, and I give the God glory for delivering me from them. There are still things that we'll go through—the reason you ask "Why is this?"

TRIALS AND TRIBULATIONS

We go through the trials and tribulations, mountains and valleys, but be reminded of this, in Psalm 23, it says, "Though I walk through the valley of the shadow of death, I will fear no evil." Take a look at that. David is saying "as I walk through," not stop, hang out, camp out, die there, lay down, or mingle. NO! He says 'I walk through the valley of the shadow of death.' Death is surrounding him. The situations are not the best. He says, "I will fear no evil" There's a key there, and I hope you grab it. He says "I will fear no evil." You see, fear opens the door to the enemy that paralyzes us. It causes us not to follow through the fullness of what God wants us to have. I will fear no evil, David says. Why? "Because of your rod and your staff, they comfort me."

What we just took from that, in Psalm 23, is so important. Our happiness and our peace are in the Lord. Our power is through the Holy Spirit. Our Lord, His rod and His staff, they comfort us. Jesus said, "Go and do what I did and even greater." And then, He made a standing proclamation. He told them, "Wait until the Holy Spirit comes upon you to go in ministry." This is important because the Holy Spirit is the Spirit of truth, the Great Counselor. He is the One who brings peace, hope, joy and love, to name just a few of the nine gifts that He has for us.

THE BATTLE TURNS

I hope you're encouraged so far in this book, and I hope that you take encouragement as we enter this part of my life. The tide of the battle turns as I start walking more in my call to ministry, so let's get to the story here.

A CALL TO ACTION

It was an afternoon, as I was at my small house that I resided in at Humble, Texas. I received a phone call from my biological father, Ron Simmons, asking for prayer for little Elena. She was my niece to my step sister Julie. Little Elena had been through so much in her life ever since her birth. So many times, they have spoken death over her, but God. The reality is many miracles have already taken place in her life. She was about four years old at this point.

As my biological father communicated on the telephone with me that she had been in the hospital and they did not know what was wrong with her, but it had the potential to take her life. I immediately stood in agreement and said, "Yes, we will pray." The Holy Spirit came upon me in such a measure that I knew I needed to travel to Ripley, Tennessee, to lay hands on little Elena. The Holy Spirit communicated with me to contact my friend Blake. As I touched base with Blake through a telephone call, he agreed that he had a witness from the Holy Spirit to go. It all sounded great so far, but there were a few challenges—a few challenges that would probably stop most people today from going forward. I knew that the Holy Spirit had said to go forward and that's what we're going to do.

You say, "What were the challenges, Richard?" I'm glad you asked. The problems included finances. We had just $45, and we had to travel from Humble, Texas, just north of Houston, Texas, to Ripley, Tennessee. This is roughly a ten-hour drive. It goes up to Shreveport, Louisiana, then on through Arkansas, at the Little Rock, Arkansas then up to Memphis, Tennessee. Then it is about an hour and a half drive outside of Tennessee. You arrive at Ripley, Tennessee. I knew that the Lord was saying to go and we had $45. I had $45. So by faith, we started the journey. There was no turning back, and there were no guarantees outside of full faith and trusting the Lord Jesus Christ and responding to the call of the Holy Spirit.

ON THE JOURNEY

I picked up Blake, and we went to fill up the car in Humble, Texas. After we had filled up the car, I told Blake 'Let's lay our hands on the gas gauge indicator. Let's ask God to stretch the fuel up to get us to our destination." He agreed. In fact, Blake was just as crazy as I was about the things of God and trusting God.

I think, many times, people thought we were a little bit on edge. You know, I believe, we are. I believe God responded to that great, crazy faith.

We left the Shell gas station there at Humble, Texas and in our journey, I'll let you know the Lord stretched our gas from Humble, Texas all the way to Little Rock, Arkansas. You say that's impossible, and I say that's a miracle.

At Little Rock, Arkansas, we filled up again. We journeyed on through Memphis, Tennessee to get just to the other side of Memphis where we filled up with the remaining bit of money. In fact, I don't even believe we filled the whole tank up. We just put the rest of the money in, and that gave us about three-quarters of a tank. We drove from that gas station onto Ripley, Tennessee which took about an hour and a half.

We arrived at my biological father's home, there on the coffee shop lane in Ripley, TN. It was fascinating. We pulled in with such great peace—No worries, no concerns, just trusting God.

As faithful as the Lord is, our food was provided there, but more importantly, the Lord was there. It was a Saturday that we arrived.

A VISIT TO WHITEFIELD

Sunday morning, we attended the Whitefield Assemblies of God with my biological father Ron and his wife, Diane Simmons. My step sister Julie and little Elena attended. My step brother Joey attended with his girlfriend as well.

Blake and I were probably considered radical Christians. We like to go on the edge. We like the fullness of the Holy Spirit. We've both attended the Victory Christian Center located in Houston, Texas. If you want a real touch from the Holy Spirit, I urge you to stop by at the Victory Christian Center Friday night, and you'll find the Holy Spirit moving in such a radical, powerful way that it will blow your mind. Do not just stop there, go and meet with Pastor Tony Krishack afterward. He's such an amazing man of God that poured so much into my life. Back to our time there at the Whitefield Assembly in Ripley, Tennessee, it was a Sunday morning. We were there with the whole family and the service ensued. It felt a tad bit religious – very tight, very controlled—well, to me and Blake's standards at least. They called for an altar call and Blake, and I went up and prayed at the altar as we knelt on our knees and sought the Lord out. We both had a nice touch from the Holy Spirit there and honestly felt like God had used us to pour out into the place with His presence.

I had a vision while I was on the floor of the Lord, beginning to bring a river from that altar and some gold flowing through that river. I released it to the pastor of the church, and I could tell, he was being courteous but dismissed it as this is just some guy that's not credentialed. I believe that day cost that church in a tremendous way as the Lord was trying to deliver something prophetically. How many times has this occurred across this great nation of the United States today where God is trying to bring something or bring a move and the people he is using to bring it do not look like the norm and that very thing is stillborn? We need revival in this land.

After church, we returned to my biological father's home where we enjoyed some excellent finger foods and made our way downstairs to the big television in the basement.

HERE FLOWS A HEALING

They had a satellite TV system, and we turned on *God TV* to find the *Lakeland Revival* streaming through. It was such an anointed and powerful flow that was coming through. Roy Fields was leading the worship. You want to talk about an anointed man of God who's humble; that's Roy Fields. Every time I hear him praise, I'm touched so profoundly by the anointing of the Holy Ghost. It's not even funny.

That day, Roy Fields was leading worship as they were streaming worldwide through *God TV*. We were all dancing around and rejoicing in the basement. There sits little Elena on the floor. I felt moved by the Holy Spirit to pick her up and dance with her. The Holy Spirit said, "Pick her up and dance with her." I want to dance with you. I said "Wow!" I scooped little Elena into my arms, and we began to dance. The anointing of the Holy Ghost fell upon us in such a way as if Jesus was just right there with us. It was so powerful! I kept having visions of Jesus just holding us, and I held her. I believe that day; the Lord was right there through his Holy Spirit just holding us. The passing of his anointing and bondage-breaking power healed and delivered little Elena from whatever it was her doctors couldn't figure out. After we had been finished worshipping, I put little

Elena down, and we were rejoicing in The Lord's presence there that day. It was powerful!

BACK TO THE DOCTOR

The next day, we agreed to go with my step sister Julie to the physician's clinic located in Memphis, Tennessee. As we joined her and little Elena in the car, we made the trip. We all came into agreement that it was done. I strangely knew it the night before, as we were dancing around, the Lord had touched little Elena and healed her. All glory to the Lord God Almighty!

Blake and I were sitting in the living room while the doctor saw little Elena with her mother. Lying on the table in front of me was a major magazine and on the front cover of it was a caption about the last five minutes of Martin Luther King's life. I was intrigued; I was pulled to that caption by the Holy Spirit. I didn't have a particular interest per se in Martin Luther King at that point. I'd always been a very open-minded and loving person, not being racial. In fact, for a period of my life, I had leaned more towards African-American and Hispanic folks than I did the Whites. I want to find Jesus. I found peace, love, and hope with every race knowing that the color red is what flowed through our veins. The very blood that Jesus Christ bled for each of us is red. Looking deeper at the bloodline of Abraham and how we're all in the bloodline of Abraham, we are brothers and sisters, under the adoption of the Most High God. We should rejoice in that daily.

Reading that article detailed the last five minutes of Martin Luther King's life, how he had a visitor and some of the details of his life and not being the perfect man, but having a love for God. In fact, he reminded me a lot of David.

CALLED AND CHOSEN

The Lord encouraged me that day. The Holy Spirit spoke to me, and He said "Your life has not been perfect, but I'm going to use you in mighty ways. It's going to come at a significant cost."

I said "Yes, Lord! I'll do and go wherever you want me to go and whatever you want me to do."

He told me "I called you from birth. I'm going to use you. There's going to be miles that you're going to travel. There's going to be mountains and valleys. Keep your eyes on me. You will see."

I said, "Yes, Lord. Your will be done."

WHERE DID IT GO?

Not long after that, little Elena and her mom Julie came out from the doctor's visit with an excellent report. Just four days ago, the doctor's report was that something unknown was potentially going to take her life, and now it no longer existed. In fact, she was in great health according to the doctor's report that day. To God be all the glory! That's the power of the living God that we serve. He's healing. He's magnificent! He is the Great I am. He is the Alpha and the Omega, the Beginning and the End.

When we look at His truth in Isaiah 53:5, we see this: The very prophecies set forth said that by the stripes that Jesus Christ took that we are healed and made whole. That's true for little Elena that day, and that's true for anyone reading this book right now. No matter what you're going through, call on the name of the Lord Jesus Christ and be saved. Dig into His Word. Know Him in such intimacy and let Him move in your life, healing you, delivering you, being your ever present help in times of need, and times of trouble. Remember Psalm 46:1, for that's who

He is.

We all loaded up in the car and traveled back from Memphis that day to Ripley. When we got back to Ripley, we all rejoiced and fellowshipped and then Blake and I went to sit on the back porch.

A SHIFT

As we were sitting on the back porch, an interesting conversation arose. We'd both been feeling pulled to go to the Lakeland Revival. Of course, it was going to be God because, at this point, we had no money. We were in Ripley. God has shown up to get us there. He'd shown up and healed Elena. It had been great. We were on the back porch that day saying "Lord, where are our marching orders? Holy Spirit, what do you want us to do?" As we began to discuss, feeling pulled to go to the Lakeland Revival, we both knew we need another miracle to get there. The interesting part was that the Lord had already put things in order. About five minutes into our discussion, my phone rang and a ministry partner named David was on the other end of the line. He said, "Richard, I feel like the Lord is telling me that you need to go to the Lakeland Revival." I said to him, "David, this is so confirming as I and Blake were just sitting here, having a discussion about heading there." He sent a $200 seed through Paypal, and that gave us fuel and food to move on our journey.

CROSS COUNTRY

The next morning, we left for our journey to the Lakeland, Florida. As we traveled, we went through a thousand trials and tribulations. Praise God! We had fuel, and we had food, but our GPS was coming in and out. Blake and I worked well together and by the grace of God, and GPS and maps, and ultimately the Holy Spirit's guidance, we made our way through our long journey over to Florida.

The following morning, we rolled in early to Lakeland, Florida. It was about 7 am, and my phone rang. It was a dear friend of mine, Alex, calling. He had no idea what we were up to, and we had no idea what he was doing. He put the question out there and said, "What are you doing?" Now keep in mind, Alex never called me at 7 am because I typically wasn't answering calls at 7 am, so this was an unusual occurrence.

I said, "Brother, Blake and I are driving into Lakeland, Florida."

He said, "Really?"

And I said, "Yes."

He said, "That's fascinating. I am in Lakeland, Florida."

I responded, "You're in Lakeland?"

He said, "Yes."

It was odd, downright odd. Why was it odd? It was odd because I was seeing the hand of God at work. Blake and I had about $60 left. Honestly, that wasn't going to be enough to cover for the hotel rooms. We hadn't spoken about it. We trusted the Lord, but up until this point, we looked like we were going to be staying in the parking lot in my car.

GOD SUPPLIES OUR NEEDS

The interesting thing was that Alex asked, "Where are you staying here in Lakeland?"

I said, "Brother, we don't have any place set up yet." and he responded, "The strangest thing happened. I was supposed to have a one bedroom room, but they gave me a room with two beds. If you all don't mind bunking up, you can stay with me."

Here come another miracle and answered prayer. We headed on over to meet Alex. Now the Lord had provided us a place to stay for the remaining time of the revival. We parked my car and made away downtown with Alex in his vehicle. So now the Lord had given us a place to stay and the Lord had paid for the fuel. In fact, many of our meals were paid by Alex as well.

God will supply all of your needs, guys. He's not going to tell you upfront, who, how, when, what or where, but trust Him to meet your needs. It's crazy radical faith that moves the hand of God.

As the revival went forward, one day, we were up front, and I had my video camera. I felt the Lord had been calling me to start a TV show called Lead by Faith TV. I needed to go to the restroom, but we were in front of the gate, so I just didn't think that there as a way in, but I kept feeling moved. So I responded in faith to The Holy Spirit. That feeling pulling on me, that sensing— go to the gate and ask. So, I approached the gate, and there stood a man, and he looked at me in the most interesting way; almost to be overtaken in a sense. I asked him, "Can I go through the gate? I need to use the restroom." The dumbfounded look on his face, he points to the gate, and I walked through. I honestly believe that the Spirit of God came upon that man that day.

I went into the restroom, and as I was coming out, I felt a move again—go and film some of the areas. So I went to walk around, and some of the internal areas before the revival started. I was a bit nervous, but I knew that same sensing, that same voice, that still small voice speaking to me. So I walked around filming. I could see a man at a distance, looking at me and he spoke something on his radio.

FULL ACCESS

The next thing I know, I saw a lady coming down from the top part of the stairs from the press booth. I was continuing filming like nothing going on like I don't know anything. She arrived there to me and said, "Hello, can I help you?"

I said, "Oh! Yes, ma'am. I was just here filming a little bit before everything gets started."

And she said, "Are you with a TV station? Do you have a television show?"

I said, "Yes, Ma'am. We have *Lead by Faith* television." I said, "We're just getting started, though. We haven't got to air yet."

She smiles. She put her hand out and she said to me, "The Lord told me to give you full access." I was shocked—completely shocked. Here again, God was making a way, but I had to persevere, push through and go forth.

As I went forward, I followed her upstairs to the press box where she gave me full access. I was dumbfounded. I said, "Will I be able to go down on the field and near the stage to get footage?" She said, "You have access to go anywhere you want to go." My jaw dropped because I knew this was nothing but the hand of the Lord at work.

I gathered some footage throughout the revival. On the third day there, I saw a friend of mine that I'd done some filming for earlier on at his father's ministry meeting in Houston. It is called Texas Ablaze. Troy Miller was working in his dad's ministry, Stand Firm World Ministries. So he called me from the top boxes, seeing me down there in the stand and he said, "I see you are here?" and I said, "Yes!" So we talked for a little while. He called me the next day and stated that they had to leave to Lakeland and head back to Amarillo, Texas. I said that sounds good. We'll stay in touch.

ANOTHER DOOR OPENS

So we begin to communicate more often over the next few days, sharing about what was going on at the revival and what was going on up there in Amarillo. I came to find out the Lord had directed them to put up an old fashioned tent there in Amarillo, Texas and have a tent revival meeting. He offered me the opportunity to come up and work with them in there, and I graciously agreed, seeing the hand of God yet opening another door for me. I made my way to Amarillo, Texas. It was a long drive to come into a season of working with Stand Firm World Ministries, which was a powerful and transforming time of my life. The preparation for ministry had been taking place. Now, it's time to go back. They offered and invited me to move to Amarillo, Texas and live in their intern house and work with them, but I felt moved to stay in Houston, Texas and move forward with Lead by Faith. That brings me to the next phase.

THE VOICE OF GOD

In 2008, one night I became so incredibly desperate for more of God. I began to cry out and plead with the Lord for more. I knew that there was more and I had to have it. As I laid down that night, I had put a Bible and notepad next to my bed expectant.

At 3:24 am I was awoken out of my sleep to the audible voice of God saying "You are here now listening Zerubbabel" I laid there in such a fear. I knew I needed to turn the light on and write this down.

As I turned on the light and wrote it down, I went to the bible for more answers. I went to the book of Ezra and started a journey.

It is best summarized in Ezra 5:2:

So Zerubbabel the son of Shealtiel and Jeshua the son of Jozadak rose up and began to build the house of God which is in Jerusalem; and the prophets of God were with them, helping them.

PART IV
Answering the call

CHAPTER 11

THE MIRACLE CHILD

Early Days of Ministry

From the prisons, missions fields to the ministry. The transition was now taking me to Media Ministry. I began taking some classes from Houston Media Source and, not long after that, formed a show call Kinetic TV youth in motion. It involved several young people who hosted the show, with an extensive content on pertinent topics of the time such as abortion, suicide, sex, and much more. This show had a great impact on the viewers young and old.

I had entered into marriage with Diana but realized quickly that we had made a mistake. The next five years would prove to be detrimental to my ministry from this decision and action.

In the same time, we had a home church service weekly. We moved out of our home to a small warehouse off of Lee Road in Houston and began to build. We opened and kept our hands on the plow. We were off to a good start, but the challenges would slowly start to rise.

As we continued to build, I began to see the real side of things and people. The Jezebel and Ahab spirit were on the rise. The Lord was directing me to release the people, but I was struggling with that. Having had such a hard time coming up, and overcoming, I tried and tried to help people, but it only continued to get worse. My disobedience to God cost me a season of ministry. One night as I was driving to my spiritual mother's home in Texas City to take a young man for deliverance, I received a phone call from a man named Nyron. I picked up the phone. He was weeping and said, "Brother the enemy is trying to kill you through the people closest to you and wants to destroy you." It was a confirmation of the Jezebel, Ahab and Leviathan spirits. When God says let, go... LET GO!

Ultimately, this season and disobedience to send people out caused me to become depressed, oppressed, and becoming hopeless. When the answer was just to LET GO!

A TRIP TO HEAVEN

In the midst of all of this downward spiraling, I was taken to Heaven with an encounter with Jesus one night. In this encounter, Jesus gave me a brown gift, and said through spiritual communication "I'm impounding some people in and the ministry." He then spoke spiritually and said "Revelation 1:11" to me twice. It was time for some changes.

Revelation 1:11

"I am the Alpha and the Omega, the First and the Last," and, "What you see, write in a book and send it to the seven churches which are in Asia: to Ephesus, to Smyrna, to Pergamos, to Thyatira, to Sardis, to Philadelphia, and to Laodicea."

As I returned, I began to dismantle, pray, and rebuild.

CHAPTER 12

THE MIRACLE CHILD

Known to the Unknown

God was calling me to a different place, a higher place in Him. He was continually asking me to release the people. Arguing with God is never a good thing as it only leads to frustration; and when God has left you with a unique purpose from birth, you can run but you can't hide. God was calling me to release people, but my heartache was in knowing that they were going to fall. Yes, of course, God was well aware of this, and calling me to release them so I would move forward in His plan for my life, a very special one. It would start to make sense why the enemy had tried to destroy me from birth to the days I live currently. The many time's people would just turn against me. Yes, everyday folks up to mainstream ministry- worldwide ministry leaders.

A SEASON OF SHIFTING

God always told me "If I would take care of His children, He would save my family." I believe this is an ongoing process that is unfolding, and I am looking forward to the day we are all serving the Lord together.

My mother has always been a huge part of my life, in fact,

she is my hero. From day one to now she has always believed in me and paid a tremendous price. The traumas of life tried to destroy our family, but the work God is doing in my mother now is amazing. She too has been down a rough road as I have and is growing closer to God daily. It blesses me to see her going through the trials and tribulations and calling upon the Lord God to help her come to greater wisdom, and understanding of His ways. His mercy and grace are beautiful, but His love for the broken in unmatchable.

My brother Jon who is a highly skilled contractor came out of nowhere and began to bless the ministry, and me with assistance in planning, and implementation of the forward movement of the Ministry land, and structure. Many situations that looked incredibly challenging and sometimes impossible for man but became possible as God touched my brother's heart and utilized his talents in making what was impossible very possible. I'm reminded of the scripture in Mark 9:23 "If you can believe, all things are possible to him who believes." In fact, he donated much time, labor and materials to bring it to fulfillment. My brother can be strong willed, but I have seen God touch his heart. Many times he has become a blessing to so many people in time of financial struggles. From people's roofs falling in with no way to repair it to supplying the needs of the less fortunate at Christmas time, and many other times of the year.

My biological father Ron started to become more interactive with my ministry specifically the restoration camps, and a mission trip to Honduras. To see the transition in his spiritual walk through these times tremendously blessed me beyond measure and increased my hope. It was good to serve the Lord together again, and be able to have some father and son time. My

Dad Ed always used to tell me "you need to forgive your dad Ron," and so many times it angered me, but one day that seed took root. Although we are clearly in different places in our walk, we are walking for Gods glory, and love has been restored.

Restoration began to unfold in the most unlikely ways with the most unlikely people. As God began to release Blessings upon the ministry with things such as land, financial resources, and restoration. My relationships many were either completely separating or strengthening. With my family, a restoration was taking momentum. My mother, brother Jon, and My biological father Ron began to enter stages of restoration.

THE REASON WORD

I received a word from the Lord that freed me on December 04, 2015. The word was "God says, 'the reason some people have turned against you & walked away from you without cause has nothing to do with you. It is because I have removed them from your life because they cannot go where I am taking you next. They will only hinder you in your next level because they have already served their purpose in your life. Let them go and keep moving. Greater is coming for you."

I was relieved to know that God had set me apart for a greater purpose, and I could not take them along. It made so much sense that God had utilized them as part of His plan, and I needed to let go and release them to continue in His plan.

As I released them, prophetic words would continue to come to confirm what God was doing with me.

GO MEET THIS APOSTLE

One day a periscope broadcast sounded off, and it was a

man, An Apostle from Virgina. I sensed a major pulling to listen to his show, and it was powerful. As I began to relate to the many of the topics he was covering, I found myself tuning in more often. One afternoon, this Apostle was in a conference with Dr. Matthew Stevenson, and I began to hear the Lord say "Go meet this man." I started to look for airline reservations, and was about to finalize them when I heard the Lord say "This is not the time." So I closed the browser and put it on the shelf. A week later I was sitting in the living room on the couch talking with a young man when the Lord said: "Go Now"! I began to reference his website and found the schedule. He was to be in Uvalde, Texas at a youth conference. I rented a car and immediately responded to the Lord's directions. One thing I have learned is that when He opens a door, it's only a limited time until it shuts. You don't want to be caught with the door closing in your face. When God calls don't just sit there, but respond! I departed Houston heading toward San Antonio, praying and seeking for even more information from the Lord. As I approached San Antonio, the Lord told me to call a young man Cameron in the San Antonio area. As I called him, he began to go into a deep flow from the Lord. Cameron was confirming so many things. One thing he said was that the Lord is walking you back up to the big house. In my visit to the heaven, I entered the "vineyard house" and was face to face with Jesus. I knew something was unfolding in this trip and had an excitement and expectancy from the Lord. I finally arrived at Uvalde and got a room at the local hotel. I thought the conference started the next day, so I was in my room just resting on the bed. As I was lying there, these oppressive and depressive spirits began to harass me. I started praying, and the periscope went off again. To my surprise, it was the Apostle's broadcast from the conference. I jumped up and headed to my car and took a short drive to the Uvalde

Convention Center. It was already under way, and it was alive! This Apostle began to deliver a powerful message and gave me a word, "Richard I am seeing servers downloading." I had such a witness from the Holy Spirit but had no clue what He was saying yet.

A TRIP TO FLORIDA

A few weeks later, the Lord directed me to fly and meet this Apostle at the Awakening House of Prayer in Ft. Lauderdale, Florida. It was such a great meeting with the sweetest presence of The Holy Spirit. This Apostle called me up in obedience to the Lord. He then called the prophetess up to join him in re-commissioning me.

RECOMMISSIONING

The Apostle, under the influence of the Holy Spirit, released the following over me- "Richard, come here. The Lord is mantling you in the wilderness. I re-commission you, Prophetess, come and join us. We commission you as a revivalist, we commission you as a media minister, we commission you as an Apostle to go and bring the gospel in media. We say no wall shall withstand you. The Lord has mantled you. We lose you right now and commission you. There's a sound coming out of you. There's a sound in the wilderness. There's a sound Apostle- it is something about a something about a worship leader they get their sound in the wilderness it sounded different than those who got it in the church house"

Feel free to view the video at:
hourisnow.tv/channel/richard-simmons

I am thankful for the Lord using this Apostle of God to release, mantle, and commission me again. Powerful!

A few months later the Lord told me to go to New Zealand and attend his meeting. They were powerful and ushered in an unlocking of the people and the territory. In the process, I had the opportunity to join the team on this amazing journey through Australia. It was such an honor to have him allow me to minister as part of his team. Several times through this trip, Ryan gave words from the Lord. The words pertained to the grace of Smith Wigglesworth and walking in the fullness of it.

This matched up with a word I received before meeting up with him. I will be sharing this word soon.

After we had finished going through Australia, This Apostle invited me to join him for more team ministry in South Africa for two weeks. Again it was a great and powerful time in two cities - Durban and Cape Town. I could sense our time of team ministry was coming to a completion.

A NEW DIRECTION

The evening we were concluding our trip in Cape Town, met with many of the amazing folks who we had ministered with for the last dinner. We had a fabulous dinner at the "Ocean Basket"! As we were leaving, Dr. Gustav Du Toit asked me to join him on a walk to his vehicle. I felt a witness in my spirit and joined him. As we entered the elevator to go up a floor, he began to reach out to this lady in such love for Jesus. That moment will never leave my mind. I again saw the real compassion, a true man of God with a focus on His people. I was moved, and thankful I knew this was truly a man after Gods' heart. As we departed the mall and walked to his car, Gustav asked me if I would like to join him a week later on a team ministry trip through Louisiana, Mississippi, and California. It now made sense why one door was closing, and this one was opening.

GO WEST YOUNG MAN

As we made our way ministering through Louisiana, Mississippi, and then to California; I knew I was in the right place, time with good people. As we would be in the different meetings, Dr. Gustav would acknowledge me as Apostle Richard and a mighty prophet of God. It was refreshing to be on a team that was real with no motives. While many times in the past so many others in ministry could not figure out what the Lord was doing with me and made an attempt to demote me from whom God called, ordained, commissioned and mantled me an Apostle of God. One thing was revealed to me through the process, and that is how people can begin to depend on the knowledge they have built, what other people's opinions are, but not be moved and directed by the Spirit of God.

On our trip to Orange County, California, Dr. Gustav and I were going to meet someone he knew. His name is Phillip, and all I knew was that he was in the ministry too. We arrived at Phillip's house as Gustav finished a phone call. He asked me to go to the door and let Phillip know that we had come to go for lunch. I went to the door and knocked. There was no answer. I returned to the car. As Gustav continued his phone call, I began to re-approach the door. As I got half way up the path, the door opened. When he invited me in, it felt as if I had known Phillip for many years. I felt such peace and a deep connection. We had a fabulous lunch and received surprising revelation from his many experiences with the Lord. We returned Phillip back to his home, and as we drove off, Dr. Gustav confirmed what the Lord had been speaking to me. Gustav said, "Richard, I believe this man is your spiritual father." I almost jumped out of my skin because of the confirmation that came so quickly from the Lord.

A month later I returned to minister in the Redlands, Ca area at the Edwards Mansion Chapel, and my dear friend- Joe Delgado Junior's home. In the process, I touched base with Philip, and we were able to sit down for breakfast and lunch several times. We would have amazing conversations on the Kingdom, Jesus, The Holy Spirit and so much more. Time would just fly by. We were spending 3 to 4 hours at each setting, and it seemed that time always ended so soon.

At the writing and publishing phase of this book, we are approaching the year 2017 and amazing and powerful times are about to unfold. God is rebooting many people and is about to pour out His power like never before. His suddenly's are starting to pop like popcorn in the lives of many and many more to come.

I invite you to join me on this journey real time by the following website and social links to see what God is doing! Richardbsimmons.com

facebook.com/apostlerichardbsimmons

twitter.com/ApostleRS

PART V

Prophecies Over My Life

CHAPTER 12: KNOWN TO THE UNKNOWN

CHAPTER 13

THE MIRACLE CHILD

Words To War With

Robyn Thom Rodgers: I hear you, Lord. I hear you, Lord. I hear you, Lord. Richard, you don't know the half of what God is gonna do with you, Richard. You don't know the vastness for the Lord sees the struggles that you've come up against, even down to the finances and even that it seems like there were walls that were unbalanced and they were in different forms and you're like, "God, I'm not sure what to do now." The Lord says, "Did I not send my angels and did I not pull the walls down?"

And even now, God says, "I'm even causing the room to be made for thee." God says, "I'm closing the building that will come forth and you will, one day, declare the prophet prophesied this to me."

And the Lord says, "You'll be in the place that I have birth in thee. I already told you what I would do." God says, "I'll bring you to the place where you have your own, that you won't have to lean on others, but it will be yours," says the Lord, "because you are mine and I am in you."

And the Lord says, "I will bring the provision that I have spoken to you."

The Lord says, "I will not lie to you."

And the Lord says, "I've yielded as you have yielded to me."

God says, "The things you're doing now are just stepping

stones to the vastness of my anointing power that will also flow through you."

God says, "The things of the past that are under the blood, they are not to be remembered. Don't look back; run forward because it's a new day. There's a trumpet that you're blowing for this hour and it's gonna be radical. It's gonna be new."

And the Lord says, "It's gonna be my anointing that's flowing through you. That's what it's about. You're walking in my anointing and my power."

Father, thank you for the glory of the Lord that's upon him. I thank you Lord for he's carrying things even now.

"I'm telling you, Richard, I see the enemy and I see it came one time and almost like a bone, he tried to break the bones in your wings. He tried to break you. He tried to break your rib cage. He tried to take the breath from you to stop you from even knowing how to breath. But then, you called upon me." And the Lord says, "I'll restore what the conqueror has stolen."

Then God says, "You're still in places now of even more restoration. There's things even now that's been imparted into you and the Lord says "You're gonna soar. You're gonna fly with the eye of an eagle with my desire," says the Lord.

Now Father, let the fire, fire, fire of the Holy Ghost, fire of the Holy Ghost, from the top of his head, I anoint him with the oil of gladness and joy and I say, drunk as a skunk in oil of heaven. Drunk as a skunk! fire in his feet! fire in his belly. Put a fire on his belly, in Jesus' Name. More, more, more! Drunk as a skunk in the Holy Ghost.

Ain't it wonderful, Mary? Ain't it wonderful? Ain't it glorious? Isn't it wonderful? Come here!

NATHAN: Richard, this is Nathan, ministering and praying for you. Lord, I thank you for Richard. Lord, I thank you for who you've called him to be. Lord, that you formed him, that you designed him even for a purpose. Lord, would you reveal your thoughts for him? Lord, pour out your love and your affection to him. Lord, let him know that you love him. Lord, I pray that he would be blessed and encouraged by these words.

Richard, I was seeing this picture of a glass full of cold water and how well you place that on a wooden table or a wooden piece of furniture can leave those rings behind the damage that finished that thing. But when you used a coaster, it protects it. I heard the Lord saying that He's gonna bring the protection to you that you need. He's pouring out even that covering upon you that you need. But that not only can He bring the protection, but He can bring a restoration for those things that have already been damaged, that He can come in and bring them back to the original state, that He has the ability to renew to restore things that have been damaged, even the places that the enemy has tried to come against you, that he's tried to hurt you, that he's tried to slow you down—that the Lord can bring restoration to those things. Even the things that the enemy has stolen from you—the time, even the things that were designed for you but the enemy took them away—the Lord said He's gonna be restoring those things back to you.

And then He's gonna be giving you a thick skin that the attacks of the enemy are even just gonna bounce right off and nothing's gonna stick to you, but the Lord is gonna bring the protection that you need.

Then I heard Him saying that He's even gonna begin to stir you, that He's gonna make you uncomfortable and it's almost like when you can't sleep at night. And I just heard the Lord saying that He's drawn you to Himself and that even when you can't sleep at night, when you wake up, just begin to say, "Lord, what do you wanna speak to me? What are you trying to say to me?"

And I saw even like when a mama eagle begins to stir the nest, she makes it not so comfortable anymore. She messes it all up so there's ticks— that they be checked and there's nowhere they can lay down, there's nowhere where they can get comfortable and she's forcing it out of the place where it spent, the place where it's comfortable into the place where it needs to be, that the Lord is kind of pushing you out of the place where you've been, the place that you've been comfortable—that He's drawing you closer, that He's calling you to Himself, that He's doing a good thing within you. And just begin to turn to the Lord and say "What are you trying to do with me? Where are you trying to take me? And what do you wanna do through me?" The Lord said that He's moving you in to a new season, into a day.

And I was seeing all those game shows where they had different doors and on your left "Let's see what's behind door number one." I heard the Lord saying that He's about to reveal some mysteries to you, that He's about to answer some questions that you had, that He's about to bring that clarity, and that, you know, you don't know what's behind that door. You can wonder. You can guess, but until it's opened up, you don't know.

The Lord said that He's about to open up some things to you, that He's about to reveal His mysteries even in the spirit to you, bring you to new levels in Him, giving you a new access even in spiritual realms—that He's bringing even an increase in understanding and revelation to you.

And I saw you and linking arms with some people and I heard the Lord saying that He is bringing the right people to you. He is bringing the right connections to you. He's gonna cause you to be like a magnet for the right things—that you're not gonna draw the wrong things, the wrong people, the wrong situations, but the Lord said that He's gonna cause the right things to be drawn to you.

And I heard Him saying that the doors that He opens no man can shut and the doors that He shuts no man can open. He said good things are coming your way.

And I saw you getting into a car and I heard the Lord saying "You better out on your seat belt because we're going through a ride." And it's the Holy Spirit in the driver' seat and it was just like a yielding of your will to Him, saying, "Okay, wherever You wanna take me, whatever You wanna do, I'm in for the ride." And as you put the seatbelt on, the Lord was taking you even at a new speed to the place that He wanted to go. Richard, get ready because He's about to take you for a ride. He's about to take you to places where you've never been. You're about to experience things that you've never experienced. And He said, "It's gonna happen fast and it's gonna be wild and crazy." So, you better get in the seat, place the seatbelt on and get ready for a ride.

The Scripture that the Lord was speaking to me was Psalm 23.

It says, *The Lord is my Shepherd; I shall not want.*

He makes me lie down on green pastures: He leads me beside the still waters.

He restores my soul: He leads me in the path of righteousness for His Name's sake.

Yea, though I walk through the valley of the shadow of death, I will fear no evil: for You are with me; Your rod and your staff they comfort me.

You prepare a table before me in the presence of my enemies: You anoint my head with oil; my cup runs over.

Surely, goodness and mercy shall follow me all the days of my life: and I will dwell in the house of the Lord forever.

Man, that's God's Word for you right there. The promises that He's giving you—that the Lord is gonna bless you; that He's gonna prosper you, that even when it's dark all around, the Lord said that He's gonna cause you to shine like that city on a hill; that He's gonna cause you to come out victoriously in the end.

And He said, "Don't worry!" Continue to keep your eyes fixed upon Him and He's gonna cause even the pastures to be green. Even in days of drought, even when everything else is falling apart around you, the Lord said that He's gonna cause you to be victorious and you to be prosperous.

So, Lord, I thank you for Richard. Lord, I thank you for the great things that you've got in store for him Lord for the increase, even in the spirit realms, Lord, that you are bringing to him blessing, God. Amen!

CATHY: Richard, this is Cathy, ministering and praying for you. Father, I thank you for Richard. And Lord, I pray that you pour over him the thoughts that you think toward him. Even at this time in his life that your presence would come in reality and he would experience You and Your love and Your goodness for him; and that God, he would know that Your love never fails. I ask that He never ever grow tired of hearing that You love him with an everlasting love. And may he grow deeper in your love. I thank you for speaking a Word in season to him, in Jesus Name, Amen!

Richard, I have a picture of a truck pulling up. I just saw this big truck pulling up all kinds of wood and things on it for building, delivering, you know, whatever is needed for building, like a building. And so, what I felt God say is that, He is providing what you need to build and He will even cause provision to come to you and it will at times that just-in-time provision. And so, it's like it's already on God's thought that He knows what's needed and He will cause that provision to come. But I had such a sense in seeing that truck bringing this delivery of products that God has given you what you need to go forward and even having that sense of... You know, when you are going to build, you layout the plan and you write down all that will be needed, and you count the cost. And so, I sensed you counting the cost and knowing that there is a high price to pay. You will never be disappointed in having your faith and hope in God and declaring the things that are not is all they are. And so, God is putting that strength of faith in you. You really have the gift of faith and God is stirring you in the area of faith and not to look at what you see with your natural eye, but by the spirit, perceive what God is doing and declare what God is doing.

And then, Richard, I also had a sense of... I'm sure you've seen that picture with the finger of God coming; down it's a painting. And anyways, I feel like God is putting His... All you need is just one touch of God on your life. I mean, your body gets healed, your mind, your spirit. And so, I sense God releasing healing to you and touching you with His grace, with His healing. And there's a new grace and healing flowing to you, I believe, at this time.

I looked at Isaiah 54, in verse 11, it says:

Oh you afflicted one, tossed with tempest, and not comforted, behold, I will lay your stones with colorful gems and lay your foundations with sapphires. I will make your pinnacles of rubies, your gates of crystals, and all your walls of precious stones.

All your children shall be taught by the Lord and great shall be the peace of your children.

In righteousness, you shall be established: You shall be far from oppression; for you shall not fear: and from terror; for it shall not come near you.

And so, I sensed God's protection over your life and giving you promise, even for those that would to you as a father, those that would look to you as a father in the faith. He's given you promise for those that you poured your life into. And He will complete what He has started. He is the Author and Finisher of your faith and of their faith. And so, God is stirring you even to know that He's building something great within you. And you will be strong in the Lord in the power of His might and you will not fear for faith is within you and you know that God is near.

And so, there is even a deeper understanding and revelation of the days that had your footprint will be made larger. God will bring expansion even to what you do. And He will establish even the work of your hands. And there will be the obvious recognition of God's hand upon your life and a testimony that God did it. God healed! God restored! God provided! He is the Great Lord.

So, Father, I thank you for Richard and even for faith stirring in his heart. And I ask, Lord, that you would surprise him in this season even with supernatural provision. Lord, I pray that you would surprise him even in the area of restoration and reconciliation, that You are a God of justice and You will set the record straight. I thank you for it, in Jesus' Name, Amen!

CHARITY: Richard, this is Charity, ministering and praying for you. Father, I thank you for this opportunity to pray for him. Lord, I ask that you would cause him to be more aware of your Word, of your presence. God, the authority that you have given to him to walk in, that he would even understand more of who you are. As he ready the Word, that it would come alive to him in a fresh way that he would be continually inspired and he would be able to inspire those around him, in Jesus' Name, Amen!

As I was praying for you, I had sensed that the Word has placed in you a determination, even to run in such a way as to obtain the price. You're not someone who wants to just kind of coast through or just get by or just try to figure things out on your own, but you want to do what's right and you wanna do it with the best way, the right way. And because of that, the determination and even desire within you to do that, the Lord is even drawing you to that deeper place of understanding his will, his purpose even for you. And that there is even expansion coming to you. There's an expansion of vision, expansion of where you will reach and even how you will reach different individuals. There's even a rushing in at the Father's doing because of some situations even that would want to cause there to be almost like division or stress, but he Father is coming in and even healing some wounds, broken places, and even within individual lives to see even that thing restored and healed and set free.

And so I see the Lord giving to you understanding of knowing what to say and what not to say, even how to speak with words of faith that you would begin to see increase even of His presence manifest through your life and how it will impact many around you.

Luke 4 says,

Then Jesus, being filled with the Holy Spirit, returned from the Jordan and was led by the Spirit into the wilderness, being tempted for forty days by the devil. And in those days, he ate nothing. And afterward, when he ended, he was hungry and the devil said to him "If you are the son of God, command the stone to become bread." But said to him saying "It is written, man shall not live by bread alone, but by every word that precedes out of the Word of God."

And so, here, in this passage of Scripture that was stood out to me for you is that Jesus was being filled with the Holy Spirit and was led into the wilderness. And this has been a time where you've been filled with the Spirit of God, but yet it has felt like a wilderness experience and here's the key— Jesus is praying and fasting, but in the midst of it, he's saying 'It is written' so he goes right back to the Word. And so the Word of God is living and He's calling you to that deeper place of trusting him even in the Word and to know the impacts that you will have even as a man of faith, a man of the Word. And as you pour yourself deeper into the Word, you're going to find that there is a release that's getting ready to take place right after he fast, right after he's tempted. This is when Jesus comes into the temple and the Spirit of God falls on him so heavy that everyone marvels and then they wanna throw him over a cliff. So, imagine the range of all these emotions, the trials, the testing just in a short period of time that he faced. He is well acquainted even with the testing of our faith. And so, in the midst of the storm, in the midst of all the different things of life that God is drawing you into that deeper understanding of 'Welcome to the ministry. This is how things are." Welcome to what God has for you. And this is the time where He is calling you to take that step, even to talk towards what He's called you to. Don't back-pedal. Don't step back. Don't be afraid of even what's to come. Begin to focus your eyes on Jesus. It's like when Peter got out of the boat. At first, he was ready to go, but as soon as he steps his foot onto that water and started walking, he began to recognize the storm and stopped. What was he thinking? He probably had so many different thoughts and then, he began to sink. But as soon as he called on the name of Jesus, He pulled him right back up.

And so, I see the Lord giving to you even an understanding that this is the time to keep your focus on him. He is your anchor. He is your safe place. He is your refuge. And He is even the King above all kings. SO, maintain that course that you're on. Maintain the place that you're in. Don't waver. Don't look to the left or to the right, but maintain the course that you are on and begin to keep the focus of where God has you.

So, Father, thank you that you have put much within his heart. I ask, God, that you would continue to put a faith within him to keep the focus on you— not to get distracted by anything around him, not even the storms of life— but to remain focused on you, in Jesus' Name, Amen!

CATHY: Richard, this is Cathy, ministering and praying for you. I want to just apologize for the lateness of your word coming. And just to express that we really are sorry with the passing of my husband, Pastor Bob. It's been a challenge just getting back into some things and so, please forgive us.

Father, I thank you for Richard and, Lord, I thank you for your hand upon his life and the very fact that, God, you called him by name and he belongs to you. And so, I ask that, Lord, You pour over him the oil of joy, God, that you bring gladness to him and cause him, Lord, to be stirred in faith knowing that You will complete what You have begun in him. And I pray especially for your love to flow, in Jesus' Name, Amen!

Richard, the first thing I heard as I prayed for you a little while ago was 'Ask, seek, and knock'. And Jesus talked about, to him who ask, you know, will receive. When you knock, it will be opened to you. And when you seek, you will find.

And so, I really felt like, you know, there are times that the Lord looks at us to see if we're gonna be persistent in what we are going after and believing for the greater outpouring that He has for us, if we're believing for our family members. And I really believe God has put within you a faith to believe and to know that he will, not only hear your heart's cry but He will answer you.

And so, I felt like God said to ask big and then to seek until you find it and knock until that door is opened to you. God will make a way for you and cause you to walk in confidence, knowing that you have the favor of God on your life.

AND I felt too that you'll have a message and really a message that will speak to people and cause them to know that the Lord speaks through you. And even... One of the things that I heard was 'stop, drop and roll' and just reminded me years ago, I wrote an article on 'Stop, Drop and Roll', bringing us to that place of repentance where we stop on our tracks and we drop to our knees and we roll, in other words, with the message that the Lord brought of repentance and knowing that repentance is a gift.

And so, I felt like you will have that message of bringing people back to even the basics, knowing that we must understand even the gift of repentance. But I also think too, firefighters have that message— 'stop, drop and roll'. You will be known as one who helps people and helps to bring them to that place of safety and they will feel safe with you.

There's some that will find themselves in those places where, you know when a house is burning, and someone has to jump out the window, though many times, have to be kind of coaxed out or helped out, and I really see in those kinds of situations where people—their life is hanging in the balance and you will be there to speak the wisdom and truth to them, bringing them to that place of trusting God with all of their heart.

And then I heard these words—strength, honor, dignity, and integrity—and feel like you have such a strength in you and you have so much to add to the whole and never view yourself as insignificant or not having the guts. You have the guts and you have the wisdom. And God is gonna cause double honor to come to you and you will have many people that look to you and wanna be like you, but will also follow in your footsteps.

And Isaiah 45:18-19 says,

For thus says the Lord who created the heavens, who is God, who formed the earth and made it, who has established it, who did not create it in vain, who formed it to be inhabited. I am the Lord and there is no other. I have spoke in secret in the dark place of the earth. I did not say to the seed of Jacob, "Seek me in vain." I, the Lord, speak righteousness. I declare things that are right.

And I really had, just as I even reading those Scriptures again and realizing how awesome God is and knowing that you have the favor of God in your life and people recognize even the presence of the Lord around you. And you will be that speaker of righteousness and declaring the things that are right. You will be a voice of righteousness.

Lord, I thank you for Richard and thank you for your hand upon him and holding him, God, even in that place of trusting you and knowing that you are the Author and the Finisher of his faith. You will complete what you have begun in him. And I pray that you stir him in the area of faith and cause him, Lord, to arise as a man of faith. I thank you, Lord, even as I think about faith, I think of Smith Wigglesworth. I pray that grace upon Richard, in Jesus' Name, Amen!

NATHAN: Richard, this is Nathan, ministering and praying for you. Lord, I thank you for Richard. Lord you pour your Spirit into him, Lord. Cause the increase to come. Lord, I pray for a fresh Word to be released upon him, Lord, that wherever he is, whatever he's doing, that you would let him know that you're near, that he'd feel your love, that he'd know your heart for him, God. Cause your blessing and your encouragement to be released upon him.

Richard, as I was praying for you, I asked the Lord 'where are you taking him?' and the Lord just began to release this vision to me of this bridge being built. It was being built from one place to another. And the Lord is saying He's gonna take you from the known into the unknown, that you've been successful, that you've been good at what you've done and what you're doing. But the Lord said that He has been calling you to put your hands to a new plow, that He's calling you even out of what you've known into the unknown, into what He's got for you.

And I was even hearing at 1 Kings 19:21 where Elisha is called by Elijah and He's out there plowing the field. Then Elijah comes and calls him and in verse 21, he returns back to the oxen then he slaughters some and he breaks apart that plow to create the fire. And he cooks those oxen on the fire. Now, here's something about going from what you've known into a new thing. It's like Elisha totally cut off... If he changed his mind, he couldn't go back and continue plowing that field because he totally destroyed the plow and killed his oxen and it's just like the Lord is calling you into something to kind of leave something behind and go off into this newness that He's got for you.

I even heard this saying "Lord, if this is you, then I need a clear word." And I even saw Gideon and how he put the fleece out and the Lord spoke to him. He brought that clarity to him saying "This is me. This is what I'm calling you to do."—The Lord, saying "Don't be afraid to cry out to him. Don't be afraid to put the fleece out because He's gonna cause that clear word to come." He's gonna cause the clarity to be there, that you're gonna know that you know that this is what God's calling you to do, that it's not just you, that it's not just what you wanna do or what you're feeling like doing what the Lord said, that He's gonna let you know that 'Yes, this is Him. This is the thing that He's calling you to do.'

And I was seeing this thing where, sometimes, guys will do these paintings and they'll be painting away and you don't know what it is. It's kind of confusing and then all a sudden, near the end, they'll flip the painting upside-down and it reveals what they are painting at the whole time they've been painting this thing. But you couldn't see what it was. The understanding wasn't there because they're painting the thing upside-down. Once they turned that thing, flipped it around and brought the revelation of what it was, the Lord is gonna be turning this upside-down for you. He's gonna be flipping some things around that's gonna bring the understanding that's gonna bring the revelation of what He's been doing in you, that though it might seem like nothing was happening, that nothing is going on, the Lord said that He's gonna open your eyes, even the things that He's been doing, the ways that He's been preparing things, the ways that He's been causing, even His brush strokes like that an artist to begin to work things in your life—The Lord saying that He's been doing things and He's about to bring even the revelation of what He's been doing.

And I saw you even laying some things down at His feet. And I heard you saying "Lord, I don't know what to do with these. You are just placing—those are like ideas or plans or something that you're just putting before Him and saying "Lord, I don't know what to do with these—these things that are in my heart, these things that the Lord said He's about to breathe even some life into. I just saw Him breathing His breath into you that was bringing the understanding that you needed. It was like releasing even ideas or plans and strategies to you, what to do and how to do them. The Lord has even placed things upon your heart, but He hasn't placed that complete release of how to go after those things and how to see them happen. But the Lord is about to bring that to you, that He's about to download to you the strategy of even how to go forward in those things.

And I saw the Lord even placing His fire in your belly. And I heard Him saying that you're even gonna find yourself ministering to people in high places, prophesying to leaders, releasing His Word into their lives. The Lord said that He's gonna cause great doors to open up to you and not to worry about the details because He's gonna take care all of those. Don't worry about the 'Who, What, Why, Where, and How' but the Lord said that He's gonna cause those doors to open up to you. Continue to be faithful and you're gonna see even those great doors open. And He said that you're gonna cause His word to be released into great situations.

So, Lord, we thank you for Richard. Lord, we thank you for the promises that you have for Him. Lord, for the places even that you're taking Him, God, that you're pushing him forward into some great things. Would you bless him, God? Amen!

Apostle Richard travels the world evangelizing the lost while enjoying the gift of living a life in the supernatural presence of His beloved Father. This is why it is not surprising that one of Apostle Richard's favorite scripture is found in Acts 1:8

But you shall receive power when the Holy Spirit has come upon you, and you shall be witnesses to Me[a] in Jerusalem, and in all Judea and Samaria, and to the end of the earth. "

Called by God as an Apostle & Prophet, Richard is a carrier of the glory of God flowing heavily in healings, miracles, signs, and wonders.

To learn more about his work:

Lead by Faith Ministries you can visit the ministry page: lbfworld.com or richardbsimmons.com where you will have the opportunity to partner with Apostle Richard and to see what God is doing through this powerful ministry.

Connect with Richard

Facebook: facebook.com/apostlerichardbsimmons
Twitter: @apostlers
Instagram: @simmons.richard
Blog: richardbsimmons.com/blog
Video & Media: hourisnow.tv
Periscope: @richardbsimmonscom

www.ingramcontent.com/pod-product-compliance
Lightning Source LLC
Chambersburg PA
CBHW071452070426
42452CB00039B/1146